"*Loving Obedience* is the Christian parenting book I've been looking for! As a busy pediatrician, it is a joy to be able to recommend such a readable, understandable and practical book to busy parents who are looking for a quiet, sensible approach to raising their children in a confused society shouting anything but common sense solutions. I have used it in my own home and I am so grateful that this resource is available for me to recommend to my moms and dads."

> Harry V. Phillips III, M.D.
> Pediatrician
> Past President,
> Memphis and Midsouth Pediatric Society

"Bill Richardson's gift of communication is richly embodied in the pages of *Loving Obedience*. The Lord will greatly use this incredible tool to build His kingdom in the lives of precious little ones entrusted to those who will read these pages of wisdom."

> LeRoy H. Paris II
> President, Board of Directors,
> Mission Mississippi

"I highly recommend *Loving Obedience* to any parent, teacher, social worker, children's minister or pastor. If you work with children, you need this material. *Loving Obedience* is wonderful material that is grounded in biblical truth, easy to understand and extremely practical."

> Steve Lanier, M.A.
> Served 20 years as a Youth for Christ state director

"*Loving Obedience* is one of the most practical, user friendly, biblical presentations on parenting that I've found . . . the skills presented in this material can be put to use immediately."

> Kevin K. Hand, Ph.D.
> Senior Pastor,
> First Baptist Church, Magee, MS

D0289008

LOVING OBEDIENCE

CHILD TRAINING TECHNIQUES THAT WORK

William J. Richardson, Ph.D.

NORTHFIELD PUBLISHING

CHICAGO

ISBN: 1-881273-26-1

1 3 5 7 9 10 8 6 4 2

Printed in the United States of America

This book is lovingly dedicated
with deepest gratitude to my family:
To my patient wife
my love and life-partner; perspicacious parent extraordinaire
To my fine and fun sons
who are my laughing and loving university
To my parents
who tacitly taught me much of what follows
To my spiritual parents
who gave me the two greatest gifts
And to my heavenly Father
whose loving kindness to me,
as my thankfulness to Him, is ineffable.

CONTENTS

ACKNOWLEDGEMENTS

I owe special thanks to so many who made this book possible. My colleague and close friend James B. Hurley has always encouraged me to write and made it logistically possible *vis a vis* departmental demands. My fellow workers Barbara Martin and Alice Fulghum have labored so often to take up slack left by my writing, and they have been friends without equal, giving more support than I can properly express.

A host of wonderful student assistants at RTS over the years have been invaluable, not to mention enjoyable: Linda Persenaire, David Rice, Kathleen Womack, Judy Harris, Michele Mauchamer, Chip Pillow, Paul Gilbert, and Chandler Coe.

Two more friends and hard workers who helped me with untold numbers of book-related tasks and always with amazingly sweet spirits were MFT Departmental Secretaries Toni Kinchen and Martha Foster. To all of you I am deeply indebted, and for all of you I am profoundly thankful.

INTRODUCTION

I vividly remember the moment I fell in love with our first son. He had just been forced to leave a cozy womb, squeezed through the birth canal for ten hours, then ejected into the blaring lights and frigid temperatures of an operating room. He was not happy. He needed no swat on the bottom to start crying. He wailed with all his might as nurses cleaned, checked, and wrapped him up. He kept screaming as they brought him to me and placed him in my arms.

Then it happened. I looked down at him, and he looked up at me. He became utterly calm, just staring with big, peaceful eyes. I was mesmerized. Love for him overwhelmed me.

I also vividly remember total frustration with this same son, only a few hours later. It was his first night home. He would not go to sleep. We fed him, held him, carried him, put him down, picked him up, sang songs, read stories . . . nothing worked.

Wide awake and exasperated when the sun rose, my wife, Judi, and I did not know how to parent him through that first night. We loved him dearly, but we did not know what to do with him. We needed help.

We had received some instruction—birthing classes. We were trained for the first ten hours of labor, but we were not equipped with the knowledge or skills for the thousands of hours of parenting that would follow.[1] Who trains parents to train children?

PARENTS NEED SKILLS

Imagine reclining in your dentist's chair and hearing him say: "Well, I haven't exactly been trained to drill and fill your cavity, but my father was a dentist. I saw him do it many times. He even worked on my teeth. I think I can do it. Open up."

Think of your airline pilot making this preflight announcement: "My dad was a pilot. In fact, I sat in his cockpit and watched him fly many times. He never crashed. I'm sure I can fly this plane. Just relax, sit down, and buckle up."

Attempting such jobs without training is unthinkable. What about the job of parenting? Molding the highest of all creations into men and women who can build rockets, make friendships, and converse with the God of the universe is more complex than drilling teeth and flying planes. Attempting parenting without training is outlandish and unfair to parents and children. Yet, it is our practice.

What we learn about parenting we snatch here and there haphazardly "by the seat of our pants." Our society supplies specialized, systematic training for nearly every profession from hairdressing to aerospace engineering. But our culture, even our Christian culture, does not train us to train our children. We are not given skills of parenting in an organized, step-by-step fashion.

But knowledge and skills are available—contained in God's Word and world. Special revelation (Scripture) and general revelation (creation) hold the truths we need for training. (See Appendix A for fuller consideration of the use of special and general revelation.)

Training, teaching, or any growing is normally a rather slow affair taking place in small, steady steps rather than large, leaping strides. We learn and grow in small increments much the way that a brick building grows—one piece at a time. Effectively equipping parents means dividing the enormous edifice of parenting into small, teachable skills that help Christian mothers and fathers fulfill their call.

This book approaches parenting on a how-to, brick-by-brick

level. When we build carefully, one piece at a time, we produce an enduring edifice. My goal is to present specific skills, one piece at a time, so that parents may be built into more effective builders of their children.

A PERSONAL NOTE

Dear Reader,

I can't tell you how excited I am that powerful and effective parenting skills exist . . . and we can actually learn them. But, before we consider these skills, I want you to know three things.

First, I believe that the skills we will consider are based solidly on God's Word. Therefore, I believe they are uncommonly powerful. They will impact and change both you and your children.

Second, my belief in the effectiveness of these skills is more than academic. These parenting behaviors are a part of our home. My wife and I, though often faltering and failing, have attempted to use these skills for many years. We have seen our children benefit tremendously.

I am not boasting. Judi and I are very far from perfect, and our children share our imperfection. We are fallen and subject to all types of foolish pettiness and selfish sin. However, we have been profoundly blessed by the skills that follow.

Third, I suspect many of the parenting behaviors I suggest are already a part of your everyday lives. In such cases I rejoice, and I firmly believe that a review of these skills will enrich your household. Each time I teach or write on this subject, I too find growth in reminder.

However, some of the parenting skills in this book will be new or provide a new perspective. This delights me. My primary goal is such new discovery. In both cases, my earnest prayer is that you and your children will be blessed powerfully by what follows.

Sincerely in Christ,

Bill Richardson

NOTE

1. The job of parenting is defined at length in Appendix A. There you will also find other foundational concepts on which this book is based.

PARENTING...

is a twofold task: meeting children's needs and teaching them to meet their own needs.

To be equipped, parents must be skilled in two areas: meeting needs and teaching. The first half of this book focuses on need-meeting skills—specifically, meeting children's needs to belong and be treasured. The second half zeros in on teaching children to behave in new ways—the skills of effective discipline.

SECTION ONE:

MEETING CHILDREN'S NEEDS: SATISFYING LOVE-HUNGER

ACKNOWLEDGE ASSETS

Six-year-old Ralph was a winsome, brown-haired little fellow— a climber of trees and a builder of forts. Blessed with a vivid imagination, he entertained himself for hours as a cowboy, a superhero, or an army man. What he liked most, however, was playing with his big brother and his friends. Unfortunately, they wanted nothing to do with Ralph; he couldn't understand their jokes or play their games. And who wanted to dress up and pretend to be someone else?

One afternoon, Ralph heard his brother and some neighborhood children at the side of the house. Excitedly, he ran to join the fun. Rounding the corner, he came upon the group, some sitting on the fence, others standing—all of them towering over him. Suddenly, to his horror, the entire crowd began laughing uproariously and pointing at him. Confused, Ralph glanced around wildly, wondering, "What's wrong? Why are they laughing at me?" After what seemed an eternity, one of the boys screamed, "His zipper's open!" And everyone dissolved into laughter again.

Utterly crushed, Ralph exploded into tears. Wheeling around, he jerked up the zipper and raced into the isolation of his own backyard. There he ran pell-mell into somebody big—his dad.

Knowing exactly what had happened, Ralph's father held him

close until the sobs calmed. With tears in his own eyes, he looked at Ralph and said: "I know you're hurt, but I also know you are wonderful. I love your eyes, your ears, the feel of your hair, and the sound of your voice. I love the way God made you; He did a great job. He is delighted with you and so am I. Remember that."

And Ralph did. Twenty-two years later, he sat in my office and vividly remembered how the severe pain of rejection was dramatically lessened by his father's soothing words of acceptance.

Can you remember a time during your childhood when you, like Ralph, were teased, ridiculed, or told you didn't belong? You can probably still feel some of the emotional pain. Now change the picture. Look back to a time when you felt utterly accepted, treasured, or valued by someone or some group, as Ralph felt by his father that day. Can you remember what they did or how they did it? Perhaps they praised you or hugged you or even applauded you. You can probably recall as well the deep joy and security of those special moments.

Such experiences are powerful because God, in His perfect design, created all of us with a hunger for love. In fact, the Bible tells us that the whole law is summed up in one phrase, "Love one another" (Romans 13:9; Galatians 5:14). What an amazing "boiling-down" of all God's laws and requirements! From Genesis to Revelation all of God's directives about our treatment of one another are subsumed in one word—*love.*

And it is not just any love that we are commanded to give: "My command is this: Love each other as I have loved you" (John 15:12). How does our Lord love us? One of the many answers to this question is found in Jeremiah 31:3, "I have loved you with an everlasting love." We are commanded to love one another with a love that lasts forever. It is an unconditional, "unfailing" love, says Psalm 32:10, regardless of what a person has done, said, or even intended.

If God commanded man to give such love, it follows that God designed man to receive such love. We are built with a love-hunger. This God-given love-hunger is not unlike physical hunger. Just as we need food to survive physically, so we must have love to survive emotionally.

The same is true of our children. Their need for love is as real as their need for apples, cheese, broccoli, and bread. Without proper food they will become sick or even die. Similarly, when their love-hunger is not satisfied, they will become emotionally sick (which can also kill). *God's kind of love flowing through humans to humans is absolutely essential; it is not an optional luxury item.*

SATISFYING LOVE-HUNGER: ACKNOWLEDGING ASSETS

Parents are called to meet children's needs. Satisfying love-hunger is part of that call. But how do we satisfy love-hunger? In these first seven chapters I will give you seven different ways to do just that: one skill in each chapter to satisfy children's love-hunger.

The first skill is "Acknowledging Assets." Little Ralph's father used this method in the beginning of our chapter. It is a powerful, learnable skill involving three simple steps that can literally change the lives of the little ones who look to you for parenting.

Even though we are all sinful and fall far short of what God created us to be, we can't totally divest ourselves of the greatness of our Creator. His divine image still shines through. Though fallen, we are marvelously made. Under the inspiration of God, David wrote, "I praise you because I am fearfully and wonderfully made; your works are wonderful, I know that full well" (Psalm 139:14).[1]

Our children too are wonderful works of God with hundreds of thousands of assets. However, we lack the vision to see them. Our fallen world has trained us to miss the obvious. While we see our children's faults and deficits with awesome clarity, we are often blind to their assets. Without parental "asset vision," our children are doomed to remain blind to their own wonders. How sad—to be wonderful and not know it.

How do you go about teaching them? Use the three steps of acknowledging assets. *First, discover their assets.* Become aware of the characteristics that you treasure in your children. Assets are the "givens," the original equipment in your children that you like. You might be delighted with her red curly hair. You may find that you are quite taken by the shape of his little nose. The way she smiles may simply please you. These are all assets, qualities not acquired by any effort but simply given by God.

But acknowledging physical attributes such as the above is only the beginning. You may have a child with an uncanny memory. One of my children seldom forgets anything. I thought children were supposed to forget lunch boxes, raincoats, and jackets. Not this guy. When he was only five years old, he was reminding me to take my lunch to work. Sadly, if he didn't, I forgot. His ability to remember is a remarkable asset.

You may have a child with a sensitive heart who expresses concern for others when they suffer difficulties. Your son or daughter may display devotion for the things of God. Parents can discover countless delightful assets in each child. Make it your business to find them. Increase your asset-vision.

Second, verbally label the asset. In other words, objectively describe one of your child's attributes. Recognize out loud those assets that, in the past, you may have merely noticed with just a fleeting smile. For example, you might say:

> "Ever since I can remember, you have expressed kindness to animals,"
> > or
> "You treat little children so gently,"
> > or
> "You learn memory verses with amazing speed."

Third, verbally express your pleasure or delight in that asset. To complete the skill, add verbal appreciation. Voice your delight of the asset you have seen.

Now, combine the steps. See the asset, label it, then appreciate it. Here are some examples:

> "Your voice has deepened. It sounds so masculine; I like it."
> "Hey, your second toe is your longest. That's just like mine; I love it!"
> "Ever since you were little, you have wanted to please God. I can still see that desire, and I treasure that in you."

PRACTICE ACKNOWLEDGING ASSETS

The following is an easy exercise guaranteed to build your children. For now, choose just one of them and mentally focus on that child. Think of him or her from head to toe, from the inside of the heart to the outside of the body. Now list assets. Write down at least five "delightful givens." You might come up with a list such as the following:

Growing Taller—

"Boy, you are growing tall. I can't believe how big you've grown since last summer. It's great." What preschooler does not want to grow taller? It seems that God has made little people with an inherent desire to be big people—to grow in years, abilities, and competence. To notice and appreciate physical growth is to profoundly affirm and compliment your young child.

Glasses—

"You know what? I like the way you look in those glasses." Did you ever see a child who actually looked attractive in glasses? I have, and what a shame it would be not to acknowledge this asset. Remember, such comments must be genuine to be powerful for change.

Spiritual Interest—

"I am so pleased that your heart is open to God." From the outset, one of your little ones may have responded to the gospel of God. This does not mean that she came by sainthood genetically. She is not perfect, but this spiritual openness may have always been abundantly evident. It is a work of God in her heart and a wonderful asset to be acknowledged.

Frog-Lover—

"Nate, your investigation of frogs shows a keen interest in the world God made for you. I really like that about you." One of my guys loved frogs. He was ever searching, finding, and observing these strange little creatures. He bubbled over with a fascination for God's creation.

High Energy Level—

"I love to watch you running around, healthy and strong. God made you with lots of energy, and I like that." Parents usually want peace and quiet; we are not always overjoyed at the boundless energy in our children. Nevertheless, when they are despondent due to illness, we realize that energy is a wonderful Creator's gift.

Hand Coordination—

"Greg, see how well you can build now with these small Legos! Last Christmas you could only play with the large ones." Here's an easily missed asset. At points, children's fine-motor muscle coordination increases dramatically. Once again, God's marvelous works are evident. Abilities grow in a way that is truly, incomprehensibly marvelous. What a shame not to notice!

Please take a few moments, right now, to list assets of one of your children.

Acknowledging Assets

Child's Name: _____

Assets: _____

_____

_____

These are only a few examples of the hundreds of thousands of recognizable assets in our children. Make such a list for each child. Attempt to acknowledge an asset at least two times each day. Avoid long lectures. Use what I call the hit-and-run method. A concise, well-placed comment is powerful; the spontaneity and surprise help truth pierce the heart.

Once you begin, your asset vision will dramatically improve, and you will quickly become an expert at delighting in God's workmanship displayed in your home. It can be great fun and is typically very contagious. One day soon, your child will look back at you and say, "Dad, you sure are strong" or "Mom, you look great in that dress." While your kids are being built up, they will be learning how to build up.

WHAT ABOUT PRIDE?

But wait. Some may say, "If I acknowledge my children's assets, won't I swell their heads with pride?" I think not. The fallen world in which our children live is quite skillful in highlighting deficits and administering painful rejection.

A child's world is not an accepting place. You and I know that from observation and, sadly, from memory. Children can be cruel. Have you ever heard them cutting each other down? Our children are ridiculed if their hair is different, their bodies aren't the right shape, their athletic ability doesn't measure up—the list is endless. Our world hammers away at our children with an endless barrage of rejection. Acknowledging assets is counterculture. It's edification.

Moreover, in acknowledging their assets we are actually teaching them the truth—they are the workmanship of God; His works are wonderful. Our children will surely receive sufficient correction and critique from our lips as we teach them of their sin and fallenness and as we discipline. We should also spend time teaching them that they are fearfully and wonderfully made by their unspeakably good Creator. By virtue of His touch, they are wonderful. Their God is so grand that, even fallen, our children bear a vestige of His majestic beauty.

Acknowledging assets satisfies God-given love-hunger. It counters damage with edification. It teaches the truth. It is a potent parenting skill. Let us employ it liberally.

NOTE

1. Satisfying love-hunger is one of many essential elements in child rearing. Edifying children does not erase their need for discipline or salvation.

1. Think back to your own early childhood. Was your love-hunger met by an acknowledgment of your assets? How has that affected who you are as an adult?

2. Go through the exercise of seeing each asset, labeling it, and appreciating it. Make sure to include the different categories of the spiritual, emotional, psychological, and physical.

3. We sometimes focus on our children's faults in order to discipline them. Come up with a plan to increase the focus on assets to counterbalance negative correction.

4. Notice how your children respond to your pointing out their good qualities. Which compliments do they especially appreciate or respond to warmly? What does this say about their unique characteristics?

CHAPTER
TWO

CATCH THEM
DOING GOOD

Y ou may find this difficult to believe, but your children do thousands of "good" things every day—things that you have taught
them to do, things that you want them to do. In fact (get ready for
this), if you were to stack good behaviors next to misbehaviors,
the former would dwarf the latter—like a skyscraper next to a ranch-
style house.

Your job as a parent is to find these correct behaviors and verbally acknowledge them. Notice that good behaviors differ from assets, which we discussed in the previous chapter. Assets are the
"givens," attributes that our children possess through no effort of
their own. Good behavior, on the other hand, is a choice—when
your child chooses to do something that you taught him and want
him to do.

When we acknowledge assets, we teach our children they are
valuable, treasured creations far beyond what they do or don't ac-
complish. However, when we catch them doing something good,
we show them we are pleased by many of the things they *choose*
to do.

What are some things your children do right? Do they ever not
fight at the table? This is good! Catch them at it: "Hey, you guys aren't
fighting; I like that. Thanks."

Here are some other examples:

- Does she ever say, "Thank you"?
- Does he ever tie his own shoe?
- Does he ever use the potty?
- Does he ever take the trash out—unsolicited?
- Does he ever do the dishes without complaining?
- Does she ever say, "Please"?
- Do they ever play nicely together?
- Does she ever leave the car full of gas?
- Does she ever help her little brother?
- Does he ever get home on time?
- Does he ever call when he isn't going to be on time?
- Does she ever apologize?
- Does he ever not scream when his arm is in the headhole and his head is in the armhole of his T-shirt?
- Does he ever comb his hair?
- Does she ever say her own blessing at dinner?
- Does she ever stay in her seat at dinner?
- Is she ever angry but doesn't slam her door?
- Does he ever do his homework?

It may surprise you, but your child's day is made up of hundreds, even thousands, of little activities that you have taught her and which you want to see carried out. She gets up, she gets dressed, she eats breakfast and says, "Good morning." She has done some homework the night before, she goes off to school, she goes to band practice, she catches the bus home, she puts the milk away, she throws the clothes in the hamper (maybe), she brushes her teeth and puts the toothpaste back in its place. These are all "good" things that you taught, and she chose to do. Yes, wrong behavior is there; but the volume of good behavior is immense.

Children's good behavior does indeed outweigh the bad. I propose that the time we spend talking about those positive behaviors should be correspondingly huge compared to that spent on negative behaviors. What a radical, exciting challenge—to acknowledge the good in roughly the same volume in which it occurs.

I am not advocating permissiveness or nondisciplinary parenting. Discipline should be administered wisely, and words should be spent on it. (We will spend more than half of this book on it.) However, verbally rewarding good behavior should not be neglected.

How grievous to strive diligently and never be appreciated! How cruel to ask someone to do hundreds of tasks and never acknowledge his faithful diligence! Yet, most of our households come dangerously close to just this kind of painful oversight.

An appreciated child is a joyful child, one whose love-hunger has been at least partially satisfied. When we catch our children doing good behavior and acknowledge it, they experience a tiny but potent piece of the love and joy that we Christian parents anticipate as we think of our heavenly Father saying to us, "Well done, My good and faithful servant."

REWARD YOUR CHILDREN

In the first century, the apostle Paul, inspired by God, gave some instructions to slaves in a Greek town called Ephesus. Though this may seem an unlikely parenting context, let us look carefully into this portion of the Word of God:

> Serve wholeheartedly, as if you were serving the Lord, not men, because you know that the Lord will reward everyone for whatever good he does. (Ephesians 6:7–8)

This Scripture teaches that whatever good we do is noticed, cataloged, and will be rewarded by God. He must have quite a record-keeping system. We Christians sometimes shy away from the concept of reward, thinking that it sounds a bit selfish or self-serving. However, even a quick study of the topic reveals a Bible filled with the concept of reward. *Our God is a God who notices and rewards every single good behavior.*

Did you do anything good today? Did you make the children's lunches, go to work, greet a friend, attend church, respect an older person, treat a young person gently? All of these tiny good behaviors were noticed and cataloged by your heavenly Father. He either has or will reward you. Such notice and verbal reward is a worthy goal for the earthly parent. Since God is divine and we are human, we cannot achieve His high level of notice and recompense. However, catching our children doing something right and rewarding them is a wonderful step toward this aspect of God's character.

CATCHING THEM DOING GOOD:
A THREE-STEP PROCESS

Like acknowledging assets, catching your children doing good is a three-step skill.

Step One is to notice. Become aware of the good behaviors and attitudes as you see them. We have been trained to look right at hundreds of good behaviors and not see them at all.

Step Two is to notice verbally. After seeing good behavior, acknowledge it. I am not recommending a long dissertation or verbal discourse but a quick recognition such as, "You combed your hair . . . You took out the garbage . . . You two are playing without fighting . . . You shared a toy . . . You put your shirt in the hamper."

Step Three is verbal appreciation. A simple "I like that" or "Thank you" is usually plenty. Recently, I noticed one of my hungry children eyeing a brownie tray. Two brownies remained. One would be his and one mine. The plate came to him first. He paused, then took the smaller one, saying, "Here, Dad, you can have the big one." That was very good behavior because we both knew those were very good brownies. What a shame not to acknowledge it! I said, "Hey, you saved the big one for me. Thank you."

Catching your children doing something right can become a delightful addiction. As your awareness increases, you will see positive behaviors you never dreamed existed. Then, when your children least expect it, you can zap them:

> When you walk by the TV and notice that your hearing is still intact, you can say, with playful chiding, "You know I don't like the TV too loud. You chose to set it the way I like it. Thanks."

> Some Sunday morning you may notice that you and your spouse are actually having a conversation as you drive to church. Perhaps Susan and Michael are not embroiled in their usual backseat bantering. You can say: "You aren't fighting. This is pleasant. I love it!"

Check the smiles when you do this. Feel the family atmosphere. Catching them doing something good is powerful.

Let's practically apply this. Again, picture one of your children—a different child from the one focused on in the last chapter, if possible. Now think about the last two days you were with that child and make a list of five good things that he or she did. Please stop and do this right now in the space provided.

Catching Them Doing Good

My Child's Name: _____

1. _____

2. _____

3. _____

4. _____

5. _____

As you look at this list of five good behaviors, ask yourself, "Did I acknowledge the good I saw?" If you are like most of us, your answer to this question is probably a flat "No." We do not live in a culture that catches us doing right or that teaches us to do so. We live in a highly critical world, which expertly finds our bad behaviors but seems amazingly blind and mute when it comes to our good behaviors.

I challenge you to be counterculture. Commit yourself to seeing your children choose good behavior. Then tell them you see and appreciate it. If you commit yourself to this, you will be swimming upstream against the strong current of our highly critical culture. You will be engaging in radically different behavior. You will be satisfying your children's love-hunger. You will be taking small but potent steps toward fulfilling your children's God-given, heartfelt needs.

You will be parenting like our heavenly Parent.

1. What is the difference between acknowledging your children's assets and their good behavior?

2. Review the author's list of good behaviors. Check the ones that apply and make a note to address each one with your child in the upcoming week.

3. Now make up your own list that goes beyond the above. When you notice good behavior, make sure that you verbalize it with appreciation to your child, and don't forget to smile!

4. After one month of this new approach, schedule time with your spouse to assess how the atmosphere has changed in terms of the quality of family relationships.

CHAPTER THREE

TOUCH THE HEART

In 1945, researcher Rene Spitz made a startling discovery that has since shaped the world of child psychology and infant care. During a study of the treatment of babies in orphanages, hospitals, and the like, Spitz chose two particular institutions for observation. Both provided adequate medical and physical care, food, and facilities. He and his colleagues found the most significant difference in the child-care homes was the amount of physical attention given to the babies.[1]

In one location the infants came from "normal" backgrounds, many quite favorable. They were well cared for by a staff of about one nurse for every seven children. In the other facility, the babies were the offspring of delinquent girls, many of whom were considered emotionally disturbed or retarded. But these children received considerably more nursing care—almost one caretaker for each infant.

Spitz compared the children from both institutions at the end of one year. The infants cared for by fewer staff members were retarded in height and weight, were much more susceptible to disease, and frequently died. Compared to the babies in the other institution, these children were also regressed in their perception, body function, interpersonal relations, memory, imitation, intellect, and their ability to manipulate objects. Spitz concluded that the higher mortality rate and reduced development were due to lack of tender, physical touch.

It is no accident that God created our children to need touch in order to survive. Picture an infant—virtually all of his needs must be met through the vehicle of touch. Babies must be fed, carried, cleaned, rolled over, undressed, and dressed. God meant for our children to need touch, and He designed them in such a way to insure they would receive it. He made certain that as we care for them and meet their basic physical needs, we will simultaneously meet a deeper need for tactile stimulation—the need to be touched.

THE MIRACLE OF TOUCH

Touch can communicate when words do not. I grew up in a household with a stoic father. He was a man of very few words, especially those conveying emotion. He rarely expressed feelings of happiness, sadness, anger, or fear. As a matter of fact, I never heard him utter the words, "I love you."

Yet, it never occurred to me that he didn't. I knew he loved me, and I knew it through touch. He playfully tickled, pushed, shoved, and wrestled his message across. I received it loud and clear because touch is such a powerful signal.

Certainly, Dad was not perfect, and I do not recommend stifling verbal contact. Words are a uniquely human gift from God. They should be used. Yet, make no mistake, physical touch is a powerful love-hunger satisfier in its own right. Appropriate touch is nourishment; don't leave it out of your children's diet.

Jesus used surprising touch—at least surprising to his disciples:

> People were bringing little children to Jesus to have him touch them, but the disciples rebuked them. When Jesus saw this, he was indignant. He said to them, "Let the little children come to me, and do not hinder them, for the kingdom of God belongs to such as these" ... And he took the children in his arms, put his hands on them and blessed them. (Mark 10:13–14,16)

Jesus didn't have to touch these children. He certainly did not have to touch them in order to bless them. For that matter, He did not have to touch anyone in order to bless or heal them, but He usually did. (Please read Mark 1:40–42. When I read this passage, I always wonder how long it had been since that leper had been touched.) I don't think it's accidental that Jesus touched those children. He created the idea of tender touch; He created the need for it and the blessing of it.

PRACTICAL WAYS TO USE TOUCH

How can we use simple physical touch to satisfy love-hunger? When she is unsuspecting, hug her. When he isn't looking for it, tousle his hair. When things are quiet, tickle him. As you drive along, put your hand on her shoulder. Each time you touch in this loving way, unbeknownst to them, a nourishing, edifying surge flows into your child. They are being built up right then. Personally, I like the "sneak attack." It transforms parenting into a fun and challenging task. I like to look for unsuspecting children at unlikely moments and zap them with a surprise attack of physical affection.

Finally, we must mention one negative point about touch. It is abundantly and tragically clear that not all touch in our world is tender and nurturing. Unwholesome, abusive touch is a destructive violation of people created in God's image. It must not be tolerated. However, wholesome touch is God's design for blessing and must not be omitted.

NOTE

1. Dr. Spitz's findings were initially reported in 1945 and are contained in the *Psychoanalytic Studies of the Child* (Vol. 1) edited by D. Fenchel, et al.

1. Why do you think that physical touch in the study by Rene Spitz is related to not only emotional but also physical growth? How could something as important as memory be affected by physical touch?

2. Think of the ways you touch your own children. What message are you trying to get across? What message do they receive?

3. How do you generally combine physical touch with words? Do you verbalize what you are trying to convey? How can you do that better?

4. If your physical touch has ever been abusive or inappropriate, have the courage to discuss it with your child and seek forgiveness.

CHAPTER FOUR

HAVE SOME FUN

Having fun with your children is deceptively potent. It satisfies love-hunger. When you and your children are having fun together, you send strong relationship messages. In essence, your laughter and smiles say, *"I like being with you; you are nice to be around."*

What a lovely signal, rarely heard in the world outside your home. Outside, I guarantee they will hear, "Leave us alone ... We don't want you around ... Get out of here." Outside your home they may never hear, "We like having you with us," but they were designed for this message. Your children were made to be loved and to receive this message. Having fun with your children sends the love message loud and clear. But having fun with your children is not always an easy task to master. I have found the following three guidelines to be invaluable.

First, make sure the "fun" activity is fun for you. When my boys were three and five, they had dozens of little matchbox-sized cars and a mini-racetrack. Periodically, I put the many racetrack pieces together, elevated one end on a chair or piano, and then set up a system of hills, bumps, and jumps.

The kids loved it. Usually, their little bodies quivered with excitement as they stood in the wings watching me design their miniature superhighway. When construction was complete, they placed their cars on the elevated portion of the track and let them zoom. Seeing those cars scoot down the blue racetrack, shoot over encyclopedias, and slide under skateboards absolutely thrilled them.

But for reasons I will never understand, every time (I'm sure I'm not exaggerating) the boys ran to the end of the blue superhighway to reclaim their little speeders, they stepped on the track and broke it apart. I patiently reassembled it, only to see it smashed the very next time one of them raced to retrieve another car. I patiently repaired it again and again and ...

Within minutes I was ready to jump up and down on the wretched blue track and throw a full-blown temper tantrum, screaming, "Don't step on that track again!" By the fourth reassembling, I was gritting my teeth, rolling my eyes, and using every available ounce of spiritual resource to keep from exploding. Needless to say, I was not sending the message "I like being with you." I was sending the teeth-clenched signal "I can barely tolerate you."

Fortunately, I found other activities that were actually fun for both them and me. I think wrestling, exploring in the woods, or throwing the baseball was as much fun for me as for them. When I was enjoying myself I was inadvertently sending much healthier relationship messages.

Second, to keep it fun, keep it short. Much has been written on the children's attention span for adult-designed activities, such as school. But what about adults' attention span for children's activities? How long can one play with building blocks, Barbie dolls, or computer games? How long can one play Chutes and Ladders, dominoes, or a card game such as War? Adults probably have a shorter attention span for children's activities than vice versa. Ten to twenty minutes with a child (or children) is a little quality time that goes a long way.

Third, remove the "ruiners." Ruiners are those intruders that destroy the fun, quality times with our children. Ruiners might be telephone calls, doorbells, televisions, or the important thing you just remembered you must do.

Build a tight boundary around the fun time; set an appointment. I am a marriage and family therapist, and during my counseling appointments I don't answer the phone or catch the news. Basically, I do not allow distractions when I am in an important meeting. I recommend that you make appointments to have fun with your children because these are important meetings. During each appointment you will be indelibly teaching them that they are people who are enjoyable to be with.

It's a good idea for both parents to engage in "fun appointments" with children. Sometimes, Judi and I team up for fun with both boys; other times just one of us will play with both of them; and still other times we each take a guy. This has many implications. For instance, am I willing to spend homework time with the kids to free her for fun time? Or worse, am I willing to share housework to afford Judi some fun appointments?

How often should you have fun with your children? This is a difficult question to handle with precision. As a rule of thumb, the younger the child, the shorter the time period; the shorter the time period, the more frequent the appointment. When our guys were toddlers, Judi or I probably averaged ten minutes of fun time daily with each or both. As the boys grew to adolescence, twenty minutes once or twice a week, from either of us, was about our norm.

Let's get practical. Use the space below to list any three occasions spent with your children when both they and you had fun.

Having Some Fun

1. _____

2. _____

3. _____

You were satisfying love-hunger at those moments, unknown to you or your children. They just thought they were having fun, like children in a pizza parlor think they are just eating pizza. But pizza-eating children are being physically nourished as they devour with delight. "Fun-having" children are being nourished as they play with parents.

Use your answers, above, as guides for planning:

• Fun for you
• Short
• Undisturbed

. . . appointments that nourish.

37

1. What do you do for fun with your children, and what has made each activity fun for both of you? How has it enhanced your overall relationship?

2. Have you ever felt guilty about having too much fun? Perhaps you've put limitations on it because of a fear of self-indulgence. List the reasons you may have balked at participating in too many fun activities.

3. Talk to your child about activities you could do together in the future. Make sure that there will be some element of fun in them for you too.

4. Take out your calendar and set aside short periods for fun over the next month or months. How can you guarantee that this time together with your child will be undisturbed?

CHAPTER
FIVE

ACKNOWLEDGE EFFORT, NOT JUST ACCOMPLISHMENT

Picture an Olympics playing field—its green inner oval, its surrounding ribbons of red gravel track. Notice the stands, packed with excited people who are anxiously awaiting the next event.

Suddenly the milling crowd grows quiet. All eyes are on the starting line. A few officials gather in one area, and one prepares his starting pistol. The runners are young and in traditional garb, but as they move into position, it is evident that these are not typical athletes. Most are not as sleek and trim as one might expect. Some are actually a bit pudgy. A few wear thick glasses. Most unusual of all is the countenance of the runners—everyone is smiling, not sternly serious!

"Crack" snaps the pistol, and they're off! People crowd the finish line, jumping up and down and exuberantly cheering their runners. Here the race grows even more peculiar. The course is much shorter than normal. The runners are slow, even awkward, but the crowd in the stands explodes with ecstatic applause. Tears of joy abound as the racers stumble across the finish line into open, loving arms. There is laughter, hugging, and jumping—uncommon excitement.

Of course, by now you realize this is the Special Olympics. Are all these people cheering superior accomplishment? Hardly. No records were set; the runners, in fact, were bulky and clumsy. In this competition, pure effort was cherished and cheered, not superior accomplishment. There is a time to praise winning, but there is also a time to praise pure effort, irrespective of accomplishment.

I know a man with an extremely active ten-year-old son. It is not a severe or diagnosable problem, but the boy cannot sit still for a long time; he wants to be in constant motion. When told a story, he acts out the drama. He literally jumps up and down when he is excited. This young man overflows with activity. The attribute serves him well in some arenas. He is the ideal baseball catcher, popping up and down at every single pitch. But when it comes to reading, he has a very hard time.

One night, his father noticed him sitting on his hands as they worked together on his reading. Dad asked him, "Why are you sitting on your hands, son?" He explained, "I'm trying to sit still so I can read better." They had been reading for only about two minutes, and the son was trying so hard. It was so right to see and verbally appreciate his pure effort to calm himself and read. What a shame to miss his valiant labor, irrespective of accomplishment. His reading was rather poor. Regardless of reading skills, to ignore his diligent, persistent effort would have been cruel.

Effort in its own right is lovely and worth our open appreciation. Accomplishment should be recognized, but sometimes it will not be there. Our children will not always be successful. Effort alone is praiseworthy.

Ask yourself, "Do I really believe effort without accomplishment is valuable?" What about the little baseball player who always strikes out but keeps trying? He goes to the plate time and time again. He may never hit a home run, but can you admire the effort itself? Indeed, the courage to continue, in and of itself, is valuable.

Happily, if you value effort, you place importance on a commodity that everyone possesses. Not everyone can win the election, make the team, get an A, or make the goal. *But everyone can try.* Such effort should be prized and openly acknowledged.

I have spent many years watching children play sports, mostly baseball. I have never seen a child try to miss a grounder, purposefully make a wild throw, or intentionally strike out during a game. However, I have seen coaches and parents yell at kids who tried with 100 percent effort. The struggle to achieve was pure and wonderful, but no one acknowledged it. Those kids were wronged and wounded.

Unfortunately, such coaches and parents miss ideal opportunities to satisfy love-hunger. To see and to appreciate effort, in the face of imperfect accomplishment or even failure, is a most powerful love. It is a powerful skill for satisfying love-hunger. You can acknowledge effort when your child tries to:

- Clean up toys
- Be quiet
- Do homework
- Make his bed
- Say something nice about her least favorite teacher
- Play soccer or baseball
- Be nice to someone who is not so popular

When such attempts to achieve are isolated and treasured, regardless of superior accomplishment, love-hunger is satisfied, and your child comes to believe that she is treasured. The bedspread might be horribly crooked and loaded with wrinkles and lumps. But if he really tried to make that bed, the effort itself is beautiful. Notice it. Value it. Acknowledge it.

At our house, we have a delightful little mutt named Duncan. He is undoubtedly the sweetest, most gentle beast I have ever seen. To describe him as calm is an understatement—he sleeps all of the time. In fact, Duncan is so lethargic that we have never been able to teach him to sit up on his hind legs. We prop him up in an erect posture, but the instant we take our hands away, he collapses into a sleepy ball, staring at us with devoted and sheepish brown eyes.

One day nine-year-old Nathan decided to teach Duncan how to sit up. That day stretched into many days and weeks, always with the same result. Instead of sitting up, Duncan just melted into a puddle. I don't know what possessed Nathan to persevere in the "training," but I loved his tenacious persistence. How sad to value that effort in Nate and not tell him! I acknowledged his determination. I'm glad I had the skill.

Neither the goal nor the result of this skill is to foster mediocrity. To the contrary, acknowledging and rewarding effort frees a child to attempt new goals without fear of failure. A child learns that even when he doesn't achieve perfection the pure effort is praiseworthy.

Celebrating accomplishment, winning, and high achievement is good. However, if we acknowledge these alone and do not value effort, our children will learn that only the strongest, the brightest, the prettiest, the slimmest, or the richest are really acceptable.

Train yourself to see effort, even when its result is less than ideal. Then, acknowledge that effort and openly appreciate it. This skill, too, is very counterculture. Our society seldom values pure effort. Let us be different. Let us teach our children that they are lovely, not only when they achieve. *Let us teach them that their very effort is a lovely part of them, which we cherish.* Each time we acknowledge effort, we supply vital nourishment to our love-hungry children.

PRACTICE ACKNOWLEDGING EFFORT

Once again I ask you to interact with this material. The skill will benefit your children only if you use it. Please focus on your children and recall three instances of pure effort for each. Choose examples where the effort was obvious even though the result was lacking. Use the work space provided below. Then ask yourself, "Would I have liked my parents to acknowledge similar effort in me when I was young?" If your answer is "Yes," then share your lists with your children.

Acknowledging Effort

Place your children's names in the following blanks: _____

_____

_____

List admirable recent efforts for each child: _____

_____

_____

_____

_____

1. Has your approach in life been like the current culture—to praise winning? Do you recognize the efforts of those who don't always succeed?

2. Have you seen the results in children who are praised only for success but never for effort? What does this approach do to both children and parents?

3. Share with your children the areas in which your parents showed appreciation when you were a child. Also let them know what qualities you wish they would have recognized at that time.

4. Make a list of new areas where your children may be showing effort but it may not be sufficiently recognized. Then ask them to add their own list.

ACKNOWLEDGE IMPROVEMENTS, HOWEVER SLIGHT

In between sessions at a parenting seminar a woman stopped me. Her voice quivered with emotion, her eyes flooded as she said, "No matter how good my report card, no matter how many A's, no matter how hard I tried, my father always found something that wasn't good enough and told me I could have done better."

Sadly, this story has been told to me by many women and men. They were taught that no matter how much the effort or how great the accomplishment, it was never enough. In fact, they have come to believe that they are never good enough to be acceptable. They feel an aching emptiness inside. They feel severe hunger pains . . . love-hunger pains.

Parents don't usually foster this pain through poor motive. On the contrary, some parents genuinely believe children are motivated best by disapproval. They believe that criticism is the way to keep children striving. These parents fear that approval will bring complacency. But approval does not breed complacency. Absolutely no suggestion in God's Word or world shows that approval is stifling. To the contrary, when parents see improvements and notice accomplishment, children increase performance. In addition, when parents acknowledge improvements, children feel valued and appreciated; their love-hunger gets satisfied.

Children's improvements are a special and wonderful thing. They are ever present; that is, they are built into children. By their Creator's design, children are growing entities. They are developmental at their core—always growing. With growth comes new ability and improvement, sometimes at a staggering pace. When we see this ability-growth, we can verbally recognize it and satisfy love-hunger.

Think about the things your kids can do today that they could not do a year ago or six months ago. Can your teen work now? There was a time when he could not. Can she type now or can she type faster? Can he do algebra? There was a time when he could not. Perhaps she can diagram a sentence or even conjugate Spanish verbs. Maybe he can throw a baseball. Remember when you first tried to teach him? Perhaps he can now throw fastballs, curves, and sliders. All these are examples of improvements—some large and some small. All are improvements that can be acknowledged.

Once again, we have a three-step skill.

First, we parents must overcome our "improvement blindness" and see the improvement for what it is—a miracle of development made possible by God Himself.

Second, we verbally highlight the improvement.

Third, we express our delight about the improvement we have discovered:

> "Susan, you have learned to write in cursive. You can write all twenty-six letters. Why, I remember when you were just learning to print your alphabet. You have learned a lot."

Think about little children. Finally, Mark can pour milk from a gallon jug. This is no small improvement. When you notice, you can acknowledge:

> "Mark, good job. You just poured a glass of milk from a full gallon container. You are growing up."

Mark may not say a word. But deep inside he has heard his parent treasure him. He has heard that his development, in its most modest form, is valuable. Can she put on her jacket now? Can she tie her shoes? Can he climb a tree? Can he use a spoon or a fork? These are all improvements that can be acknowledged.

Consider older children. Can he drive a go-cart now? Has she learned to read? Maybe your teen can throw a fifty-yard pass, do calculus, or write a term paper. These are all improvements. Each of them can be acknowledged, and with each acknowledgment your child is minutely but indelibly changed. He or she has learned a small but profound truth that can never be erased: "I am valuable."

Before leaving this topic, let us observe one more thing about improvements. Improvements are improvements, no matter how slight. If his last report card had only D's and this one has a C, that's improvement. It's not great improvement, but since improvement is improvement, no matter how slight, it can be acknowledged, and love-hunger can be satisfied. No new ability is too minuscule and no progress is too tiny to keep it from qualifying for this skill.

I would like to make a request; I would like you to put your reading aside for a moment and get involved with this skill. Below, I have left you some work space. Stop and think of one of your children (or any child of any age that you know and love). Choose three specific improvements and write them down. Please resolve to share these observations with your child and then expand the skill to other children.

Acknowledging Improvements

1. _____

_____

_____

2. _____

_____

_____

3. _____

_____

_____

1. Why do you think many parents are afraid of too much approval for their child, feeling that it will breed complacency? Why is this wrong?

2. Improvement is a supernatural process, not just a natural one. When you realize that God has caused whatever growth that occurs, get together with your child and give thanks.

3. Just as you recognize effort in a number of areas, so you must learn to see improvement clearly. Find five or six tasks and measure visible improvement over time.

4. Perhaps there is one area of weakness where you often struggle with your child. Make a point of verbally acknowledging improvement, no matter how slight.

CHAPTER SEVEN

ACKNOWLEDGE CONTRIBUTIONS TO YOUR HOUSEHOLD

One mundane workday, I was sitting at my desk. I was neither depressed nor elated. I was just there, working. I paused for a break and let my thoughts drift. My mind wandered; so did my eyes, until they fell on a picture in front of me. Peering back at me from inside that picture were my two little men, my sons, Jonathan and Nathan. They were smiling at me, and—I couldn't help it—I smiled back. A little shot of joy darted through my heart when I looked at them. Then it hit me. My children make me smile and unknowingly, but profoundly, contribute to my life. It would be a shame not to let them know of their contribution.

That night when I went home, I gathered them to me for a "serious" discussion. They may have thought they were in trouble. (And I let them think so, just a little. I love to tease.) Then I said: "Sometimes, when I am at work, I think of you. And when I do, I smile. You two bring joy to my life, and I wanted you to know about it. That's all. See you later."

I hugged them both. They walked away a bit bewildered, but appreciated, nevertheless. I believe some of their love-hunger was satisfied at that moment.

The skill is simple. Look for the contributions your children bring to your home and life, then acknowledge the contributions and appreciate, out loud:

- Does he clean the pool?
- Does he mow the lawn?
- Does she make her own lunch?
- Does she clean her own car?
- Does he do the dishes?
- Does she wipe the counter with a sponge?
- Do they simply supply laughter?

If any of these activities save you time, free you for other jobs, or just enrich your home, they are genuine contributions. Acknowledge them as such, frequently. Each time you acknowledge contributions, you will be teaching them that they are valuable and that they fulfill an important function in your home. Sending such a message satisfies love-hunger.

I am confident that your children genuinely contribute to your household, regardless of their age or ability. They are made by God. It is simply not like Him to make noncontributing parts. Consider the world He has made. Its parts contribute to one another in countless examples. Animals contribute carbon dioxide to the air with each exhaling breath. Plants take in that contributed carbon dioxide to survive. Plants, in turn, contribute oxygen-rich air by which animals live. On and on goes the list of contributing creations.

God's Word directly teaches that all things contribute. Consider 1 Corinthians 12:14–22. In this passage, Paul writes of the usefulness and necessity of each part of the body. He even notes that the seemingly weaker parts are, in fact, indispensable.

Let's get personal. What about the seemingly weaker parts of your family? How do your children contribute to your household? Pause now to carefully consider your youngest child. Think of the ways in which he or she contributes to you and your home. Use the space provided to list some contributions. I will supply a few examples from past seminars. You complete the list with your youngest in mind. Later, make similar lists for your other children. Then, communicate your lists, a little at a time. Your kids will be built up as they see their value from your perspective.

Acknowledging Contributions

Youngest Child: _____

1. A four-year-old who goes to bed when we ask. Her obedience contributes peace to our home each evening.

2. A seven-year-old who wakes on his own each morning and gets himself ready for school. This makes the day much easier for Mom and Dad. It's a genuine contribution.

3. A twelve-year-old starts the lawn mower and mows the backyard upon request.

4. _____

_____

5. _____

_____

1. Just as the author shared with his children that they made him smile, find one simple and commonplace contribution that each of your children makes to your personal life. After writing your answers, share your discoveries with each child.

2. Just as Paul discusses how each member contributes to the body of Christ, list how each of your children contributes to the good of your whole family. Share this list with your children individually or corporately. (If corporately, make sure each list is equal in length and significance.)

3. Start with your lists from item #2 above and creatively project into the future (or describe the present, if applicable) to answer this question for each child, "I wonder how might God use you someday to contribute to His body, the church?"

THE LOVE-
HUNGER TEST

Now we have seen seven skills that satisfy love-hunger:

- Acknowledge assets
- Catch them doing good
- Touch
- Have some fun with your children
- Acknowledge effort
- Acknowledge improvements
- Acknowledge contributions

I call them skills for three specific reasons.

First, skills refer to craftsmanship, and parenting is the ultimate craft. Parents are craftsmen, molding and shaping the highest of all God's creation into works of untold excellence and beauty. We need skill for such a craft, and there are skills available.

Second, the designation "skill" is fitting because skills can be learned. We have more than mere hope that our handiwork will turn out well. We have much more assurance. We can learn these skills, apply them, and see our children grow in healthy self-esteem.

What joy and great relief. These are learnable skills. We can learn to edify.

Third, I call them skills because skills improve with practice. Whatever its level of effectiveness, a skill always becomes more potent with exercise. We can always grow in our ability to mold our beloved handiwork—by practicing the skills of our craft.

As you practice these seven skills, *they will sharpen.* As you continue to practice, you will see changes in your children. I guarantee it. To test my positive prediction, try this "Exercise Program." Practice one different skill each day for seven consecutive days:

- On Sundays acknowledge assets.
- On Mondays catch them doing good.
- On Tuesdays touch the heart.
- On Wednesdays have some fun.
- On Thursdays acknowledge pure effort.
- On Fridays acknowledge improvements.
- On Saturdays acknowledge contributions.

Continue the practice for three weeks. At the end of three weeks you will see the flourishing you are fostering by satisfying love-hunger.

1. Have you truly looked at parenting as a skill to be developed and practiced? Or do you see it more as just a role you play that is spontaneous?

2. How do you define "craftsmanship" as opposed to merely performing a function or playing a role? What does the former imply in terms of special skills?

3. How does the shaping of children differ from the shaping of objects or ideas? What complexities are found in the former that are not found in the latter?

4. Go back after the three-week period described above and measure two things: (1) which skill did you feel you were best at, and (2) which skill was most beneficial to your child?

CHAPTER
NINE

THE IMPOSSIBLE
COMMAND

I close this section by recounting a shocking experience. One day I was peacefully enjoying a quiet time in Ephesians chapter 4. Suddenly I was blindsided by verse 29:

> Do not let any unwholesome talk come out of your mouths, but only what is helpful for building others up according to their needs, that it may benefit those who listen.

I was awestruck when I realized this command applied to my parenting (and "husbanding" for that matter). I questioned, "Don't let *any* destructive talk come out of my mouth? Is *all* my conversation to be beneficial and building?" I believe the Author's amazing answer is, "Yes, I want all of your words to build and benefit My little ones living at your house."

But what about times when I am angry, insulted, disciplining, or just plain tired? Must my words meet my children's love-needs at all times? Again the answer is, "Yes, all your words should bless." This is a staggering command. Impossible!

In spite of a fervent love for my children, I fall so far short of this godly directive that I shudder. Other parents I know have a similar reaction. We all fall grossly short of the mark. Such a profound love is simply beyond us.

Yet, the verse stands. The prospect of using our words as constant sources of building and benefit to our children is spectacular, but, sadly, impossible.

However, there are other verses that encourage:

> Now to him who is able to do immeasurably more than all we ask or imagine, according to his power that is at work within us. (Ephesians 3:20)

Here is comfort. The same power that raised Christ from the dead is in you and me. The same power that formed and still orchestrates the billions of planets in our universe is in us. By His grace we can love with His love.

The message from these Scriptures is this: Parenting is a spiritual task. To parent the way God intended, to love our children with the love they need, we must have the power of God, and He can give us this power. Only with a moment-by-moment supply from our heavenly Father can we satisfy their love-hunger. *Vital, consistent love for our children can only come from a vibrant, consistent relationship with our Father.*

While skills training is the primary thrust of this text, we must stay ever mindful that we need the power of God's love always operating in the midst of our skills. If we do not submit to the Holy Spirit's work—if our skills are not electric with His love—we are only resounding gongs or clanging cymbals.

1. Think back to words spoken or actions taken toward your child in the past that have been unwholesome or destructive. What was the main cause—tiredness, faulty discipline, or something else?

2. Consider your list of causes above. How can you bring these moods, circumstances, and so on, under the control of the Holy Spirit?

3. How does your own walk with God affect your ability to meet your child's love-hunger needs? Allow the power of His love to speak for the benefit of your child's needs at all times.

4. Upon conclusion of this first section, what are the areas in which you find it difficult to meet your child's love-hunger needs? Try the seven skills again, and try this prayer: "Lord, fill me with Your holy love for Your children in my house."

PARENTING...

is meeting children's needs and teaching them to meet their own needs.

We now turn our attention to the second part of this parenting definition: teaching. When we address teaching we actually address discipline. Discipline is teaching children to behave in new ways.

DISCIPLINE:
TEACHING
CHILDREN TO
BEHAVE IN
NEW WAYS

PARENTING
AS TEACHING

Discipline—training or experience that corrects, molds, strengthens, or perfects
— *Webster's Third New International Dictionary*

Parents are teachers. And there is no more potent Scripture on teaching children than Proverbs 22:6: "Train up a child in the way he should go: and when he is old, he will not depart from it" (KJV).

CHILDREN NEED TRAINING

This passage stores a wealth of teacher education for parents. First, note the obvious: God tells us to train our children because *children need training.* Our children must learn hundreds of thousands of behaviors and attitudes. In other words, hundreds of thousands of behaviors and attitudes are simply not a part of their original equipment. They did not come genetically programmed to:

- Say please
- Brush teeth
- Do homework

- Mow grass
- Use a potty
- Be kind
- Treat others respectfully
- Say their blessing
- Wash their face
- Pick up shoes
- Hang wet towels
- Talk to their God

God tells us to train them because they need training in the billions of behaviors required in life.

Some secular psychologies have told us that children are flowers. With sufficient nurturing they will simply blossom into responsible, kind adults. Not so. Children need teaching in the countless behaviors, concepts, and attitudes of life. They need our guidance.

THE JOB OF THE TRAINEE

Not long ago, on an airplane, I noticed a small metal label on the stewardess's lapel: "Trainee." I remember thinking that her label advertised she was not expected to do everything right. We passengers should be tolerant. Her role was to be young and inexperienced, to *not* know how to do everything. That is the job of all trainees: to *not* know how to do everything right. Their "job" is to be inexperienced and do some things wrong.

Our children are trainees. How are they doing at their job? Are there many things they do not do right? Certainly, that is their job. Our job as trainers is to know how to live successfully and to teach our children to do the same. Their job is to *not* know how to do it— even to do it wrong—and typically they do their job rather well. Proverbs 22:6 cautions us to remember that our children are trainees. We can expect their inexperience. They will often do it just wrong.

CHILDREN ARE LEARNERS

Mom was putting on a jogging shoe that was laced up too tightly. As she tried to squeeze her foot into too small an opening, she muttered an expression of frustration, "Stupid shoe!" Two days later she walked by the room of her four-year-old. He was unsuccessfully trying to squeeze his foot into his sneaker. You can guess what she heard. "Stupid shoe!" erupted from the mouth of her sneaker-pulling four-year-old.

It's frightening the way they learn. Your kids can quote commercials, favorite movies, and unfavored teachers. (Strange that they can recite jingles but not geography.) The problem is not that children do not learn; to the contrary, they learn too much, too quickly.

The point of the proverb is this: Children are learners par excellence. Note the text "When they are old, they will not depart from it." The resounding implication is that they learn. When they are old, they will not depart from it because they learned it.

God made our children to be learners. They are sponges. They are ever soaking in and retaining data from their environment. A natural, God-designed feature is that children are always learning.[1]

Since children never stop learning, we are always teaching. When we hug them and kiss them good night, we are teaching them something. When they see us kneeling and praying in the morning, we are teaching them something. When we tell them to take out the trash and then do it ourselves, we are teaching them something. Our children are always learning something from us; we are always teaching. *In fact, we cannot not teach.* The implications of this are exciting and also frightening. Either purposefully or accidentally, we are always teaching, and they are always learning.

THE TIME OF LEARNING

Children are always learning, but lest we become overly optimistic, thinking this parenting-teaching is a snap, let us make one more observation on the proverb: "When they are old, they will not depart from it." I wish it read, "As soon as they hear it, they will immediately incorporate it." Some learning happens on the spot and sticks. Sometimes, discipline may take a few days to bring change, sometimes it may take weeks. Some learning can take a lifetime. In fact, we may never see some of our good teaching realized in our children; however, the sown seed will grow and blossom.

I write this to encourage. Your efforts will change your child, but the time of learning will vary. They benefit from your teaching. Sometimes you will see and enjoy the fruit. Some results may not bloom until later years.[2]

We have seen some powerful parenting insights in Proverb 22:6.

- Our kids don't come originally equipped with the billions of behaviors necessary for life. They need training.
- They are trainees, and we can expect them to do it wrong for a while.
- Our children are always learning something from us—we can't not teach.
- Our teaching will inevitably affect our children.

The bottom line is that our kids are ever learning, we are always teaching, and our teaching dramatically affects their lives, even their eternities.[3] *Yet, we are teachers without training.* As I noted on the first pages of this book, our society supplies specialized, systematic training for nearly every profession from hairdressing to aerospace engineering. But our culture, even our Christian culture, does not train us to train our children. The parenting-teaching job is not only immensely complex, it is of immediate and eternal significance. We need training!

What follows is an attempt to supply some organized, systematic teacher training for parents.

NOTES

1. At this point we parents ask, "Why is it that my little sponge does not hear me tell him to go to bed until I yell it the fifth time?" Unfortunately, that particular little absorber has probably learned that we will not "consequentially" enforce bedtime until after the fifth yell. But there is much more on this in chapter 14.
2. Much more can be learned about parenting from Proverbs 22:6. For example, "In the way that he should go" is probably better rendered, "according to his or her own unique style." For further useful considerations, I refer you to *Your Child's Hidden Needs,* by Bruce Narramore, and *You and Your Child,* by Charles Swindoll.
3. Leading our children to a saving knowledge of Jesus Christ is influenced greatly by the ways we satisfy their love-hunger and discipline them, the topics of this book. Their salvation is a topic so important that it deserves full and careful attention in a book(s) of its own.

1. Review the lists of learned behaviors that do not come naturally to your children. Try to make your own list of learned attitudes that children need to acquire to become mature adults.

2. Now draw up a list combining both wrong attitudes and wrong
   behaviors that from time to time your child exhibits. How can
   they be replaced with their positive counterparts?

3. We always teach our children by what we do and who we are.
   When have your actions not matched up to the words as you
   taught your children?

4. What types of learning on your child's part take only minutes?
   What other types of learning may take months or years? What
   insight does this give you concerning your child?

CHAPTER ELEVEN

THREE LAWS
OF LEARNING

We begin teacher training for parents by considering three things all teachers must know—three laws of learning.

My wife, Judi, and I were walking down a tree-shaded, lakeside path. It was rolling and dotted with little bridges. As we walked we heard a little person trotting up behind us. She was about four. When she jogged past, we heard her mother, a good ten yards back, huffing and crying out, "Susan, wait. Stop running!" Susan gleefully giggled and continued her morning exercise. Mother continued to chase, but her pleading took on a menacing tone: "Susan, stop right now." Still giggling, Susan disappeared down the path and over the hill. As Mom passed us, she gained on Susan and began yelling.

The chase continued. Finally, we saw Mom overtake Susan. Her concern vanished. She swept Susan up in her arms, tickled her, and playfully exclaimed, "Oh, Susan, you must listen to Mother, you little bugger." Both laughed aloud. I am confident that little Susan played this "game" again soon. Susan and her mother were illustrating the first law of learning.

THE FIRST LAW OF LEARNING:
IF IT WORKS, IT HAPPENS AGAIN

It worked for Susan. There was great positive consequence for running away from Mother and ignoring her command to stop. It paid off. Susan received warm and laughing hugs as a reward for her flight and refusal to obey. Mom's words *told* Susan to listen. Her actions *taught* Susan to ignore. Susan's mother was teaching her to disobey.

Picture a teen. He is fifteen and leaves piles of dirty clothes wherever he happens to step out of them. His mother hollers, "Jeff, do not leave your clothes lying around," as she picks up those clothes and puts them in the hamper. What is Mom really teaching? What will Jeff do the next time he steps out of his crumpled clothing? If it works, it happens again . . . and it works for Jeff to leave his clothes on the floor. When he does, they are "magically" removed, hampered, laundered, and replaced.

This last example is from my own home. Nathan was about three years old. Judi and I were putting him and his big brother to bed; they shared a room at the time. We talked a little, said prayers, kissed good night, then Judi and I left. We draped ourselves over living room furniture, tired from a full day. Suddenly, Nathan screamed with a loud and terrible shrill. We bolted back to his room expecting to see bloody, maimed children. I got there first. With wide eyes Nathan exclaimed, "There are monsters outside my window." I was relieved that it was only "monsters," not maiming, but also concerned for his fear. I gathered him up in my arms and with gentle voice said:

> "Oh, Nate, there are no such things as monsters. And besides, Jesus is here with you; He is the strongest Protector of all. He made the whole world. Jonathan is right here, so you are not alone. [Jonathan was, somehow, sleeping through all of this.] Mom and I are in the very next room. We'll take care of you."

I carried him outside and showed him that there were, in fact, no monsters. It was a fine summer eve. I sat on the cool grass. Nathan was on my lap. I was his sofa. We leaned back, looked at the beautiful sky, and talked about God and stars. It was a great moment of warm relationship. I brought Nathan back in, laid him in his bed, scratched his back, said prayers again, and he soon went off to sleep with calm on his face. All was well.

The next night Judi and I put the boys to bed, said prayers, and made our way to peacefully collapse in the living room. A blood-curdling scream came suddenly from Nathan's room. I galloped to his bedside. He had the same wide eyes as before. "There are monsters outside my window."

I held him and spoke softly, "Nate, there are no such things as monsters . . . Jesus is here . . . we are in the next room." I carried him outside. We looked at stars. I brought him in and continued the same routine as the night before.

As Nathan and I sat on the lawn the third night discussing the stars, I began to suspect that something was not right. It dawned on me that I was teaching him to be afraid. If it works, it happens again. A little guy gets frightened, Dad rushes in, holds him, and gives words of comfort. Next comes an outdoor excursion. Finally, a brief, biblical astronomy lesson is topped off by a bedside massage. Not a bad evening.

I realized the extent of the benefit earned by Nathan's fear. Further, I realized that though my words said, "There are no monsters," my well-intended actions said, "If you allow fear to overwhelm you, nice things will follow." I was teaching Nathan to allow fear to well up and control him.

How was I to "unteach" Nathan's fear? That specific teaching skill is the topic of the next chapter. So tune in there for the continuing saga of Nathan's moonlight monsters.

Practicing Law Number One

Take a moment, right now, to stop and think of a problem behavior in one of the little ones (or not-so-little ones) in your home. Label a behavior that he or she keeps doing. For example:

- She runs to her room and slams her door in anger.
- He throws tantrums.
- She consistently comes in late.
- She argues with you when you ask her to do a chore.
- He ignores you when you call his name.

DESCRIBE THE PROBLEM BEHAVIOR:

_____

_____

Now, try to find the benefit. What positive consequence keeps this behavior going? If you look hard enough, you will find it. It may not occur every time, but somewhere there is a benefit. Ask yourself what happens immediately after the tantrum. What happens immediately after she argues or just after he ignores? Find the probable benefit and list it below.

DESCRIBE THE POSITIVE CONSEQUENCE:

_____

_____

With a little effort, you will probably find positive consequences that reinforce problem behaviors. Like Nathan's fear, these behaviors will be followed by some pleasant experience. If it works, it happens again. Your insight into the positive consequence of the negative behavior will be a key to teaching your child.

THE SECOND LAW OF LEARNING: LEARNING IS A TWO-STEP

Learning always involves two steps: stopping old behaviors, then starting new ones. A child never just learns to eat with a spoon. That would be hard enough. No, she must first *stop* scooping up the mashed potatoes with her hand (the old way) and *start* trying to grasp, scoop, and balance the mashed potatoes with this thing called "spoon." Similarly, she will not just learn to use the potty someday. She must stop using the all-convenient diaper and start using the potty.

A teenager does not just learn to hang up wet bath towels. First, he must *stop* what he is presently doing—just dropping them on the bathroom floor. Then he *starts* something novel—hanging up the wet towels.

All learning is a two-step process. We must stop one comfortable behavior, such as lashing out in anger, in order to start a new foreign behavior such as talking calmly about grievances. Learning is always a two-step.

If learning is a two-step, so is teaching. Teaching our children always means teaching a child to stop one behavior and then teaching them to start another. Distinguishing between the behavior to be stopped and the behavior to be started is absolutely crucial, because *the methods of teaching children to stop are very different from the methods of teaching children to start.* We must be clear about what our children are to stop and what they are to start so that we can apply the right method at the right time.

Practicing Law Number Two

Michelle's parents are concerned. She is six years old and seldom, if ever, says, "Please." Her parents would like to teach her to say, "Yes, please," when she is offered something she wants. Use the space provided below (and your imagination to fill in a few details) to label the behavior Michelle should stop and the behavior Michelle should start.

BEHAVIOR TO BE STOPPED:

_____

_____

BEHAVIOR TO BE STARTED:

_____

_____

When her parents ferreted out which behaviors they wanted Michelle to stop and which they wanted her to start, they arrived at the following:

BEHAVIOR TO BE STOPPED:

Just taking food or toys that people offer and silently going about her business.

BEHAVIOR TO BE STARTED:

Saying, "Yes, please," and then receiving the item offered, if she wishes to receive it.

Earlier in this chapter, you specified a problem behavior. Please refer to that problem behavior now, and use the space below to specifically label what behavior you would like your child to stop and what behavior you would like your child to start.

BEHAVIOR TO BE STOPPED:

BEHAVIOR TO BE STARTED:

THE THIRD LAW OF LEARNING:
SMALL BITES CHEW EASIER

Trying to tackle too many discipline issues at once is like trying to teach a first grader addition, subtraction, multiplication, and division all at the same time. Learning to play tennis, basketball, baseball, and soccer in the same season is too much. Small learning tasks are simply more learnable. Students are encouraged. Teachers are encouraged.

As a rule, we do not learn large, complicated concepts or behaviors. We learn best by systematically mastering small steps, which later combine into more complex skills. We do not first teach a child to say, "Peter Piper picked a peck of pickled peppers." We start more humbly with learnable words such as "da-da" and "mama." Break learning down into easily learnable components. Do not teach that fifth grader to be an honor-roll student—teach him to learn five spelling words each night.

Practicing Law Number Three

Terry and Tommy are eight-year-old twins. Their parents are perturbed. They agree that the twins are rude to adults. But asking the boys to stop being rude and start being more polite is too general and vague. These parent-teachers wisely chose the specific location of "church" and focused on smaller, specific behaviors.

SMALL, SPECIFIC BEHAVIORS TO BE STOPPED:

Looking down and saying nothing when greeted by adults at church.

SMALL, SPECIFIC BEHAVIORS TO BE STARTED:

Making eye contact and saying, "Hello," to adults at church who greet you.

This real-life example of increased clarity had astounding impact. Soon, the twins' new behavior spread to other places and persons. To foster successful learning, specifically focus on doable behaviors, then branch out.

Once again, refer to the problem behavior you identified above. Carefully consider this problem and attempt *to narrow it down to one or two small behaviors* that you would like stopped and started. Be as specific as possible.

SMALL, SPECIFIC BEHAVIORS TO BE STOPPED:

_____

_____

SMALL, SPECIFIC BEHAVIORS TO BE STARTED:

_____

_____

THREE LAWS OF LEARNING[1]

We have considered three essential principles:

- If it works, it happens again.
- Learning is always a two-step.
- Small bites chew easier.

These laws permeate all that teachers do. Standing firm on this triple foundation, we are ready to see and use the skills of discipline in the following chapters.

NOTE

1. These three laws of learning directly form the fabric of the discipline skills which follow. An additional learning principle always at work, and useful to remember, is modeling, i.e., people learn through imitation. In varying degrees children imitate parents, siblings, peers, TV, radio, etc.

1. Consider again the story of Nathan and the monsters. Under what circumstances have your loving attempts to help your child only reinforced the negative behavior?

2. Make a list of four problem behaviors in your child's life that need to stop. In a second column, write out the corresponding behavior that needs to start. Be as specific as you can.

3. As you review these two columns, describe in your own words how you would use different teaching methods for stopping one kind of behavior and starting another.

4. Based upon the "law of bite-sized chunks," choose one problem behavior and its corresponding desired behavior. Then plan how you could stop the one and help your child start the other.

CHAPTER
TWELVE

TEACHING CHILDREN TO STOP: REMOVE THE BENEFIT

Teaching is a two-step. First we teach children to stop the old, unwanted behavior. Then, we teach them to start a new behavior. In keeping with this logical order, let's first consider skills for teaching children to stop. The next three chapters cover three such skills. Our first skill for teaching children to stop is simply stated as follows:

Remove the benefit to stop the behavior.

Some behaviors respond beautifully to this skill. The undesired behavior simply dissipates when it no longer pays off. Nathan's monster story from chapter 11 is a case in point. Now, the rest of the story.

Nathan's behavior was new, not a long-term habit. There appeared to be no deep and hidden reasons for his behavior (no traumas in his life giving rise to the fears). So this is what we did.

Prior to lights-out on night number four, I said this to four-year-old Nathan:

"Nate, if you should get scared again tonight about monsters, don't worry. I know you will be safe. There are no monsters. Besides, Mom and I are just in the next room, and our Lord, the Great Protector, is right here with you. I am not afraid you will be harmed. You won't be—you'll be fine. In fact, I am not even going to come into your room if you get afraid, because I know there is nothing here to hurt you. You will be just fine. Good night, my son."

Three to five minutes of silence filled our anxious household that night after prayers. Judi and I sat on pins and needles in the living room. Then it happened as predicted; Nathan cried out. He sounded scared. I walked back to peek in undetected, making sure he was not physically injured this time. He was fine, and I returned to the living room to sit down and miserably listen to four unbelievably long minutes of crying. Finally, he was quiet. I went in—he was asleep.

The next night I miserably listened to about three minutes of my little son's fearful cry. Night number three held only about sixty seconds of fear for him. Night four to the present have been calm and peaceful for Nathan. He does not believe that there are monsters outside of his window. When the benefit was gone, Nathan's fear was soon gone.[1]

THE CASE OF THE INFANT INSOMNIAC

Two fine Christian parents came to see me after viewing a television program on childhood sleeping disorders. Their first child, a nine-month-old, was their concern. He was still waking every two to three hours during the night.

Babies need to be held, cuddled, and fed. In a word they need to be "babied." However, if it works, it happens again, and a nine-month-old will continue to cry just for the benefit of it—the late-night company. Holding, feeding, and touching is a very positive consequence.

You can guess the remedy. After gathering some behavioral and medical data from parents and pediatrician, we tried removing the benefit.

"Feed this fine baby, change him, and put him to bed at 10:00 P.M., but do not go to him at 1:00 A.M. You'll certainly hear him, but let him cry through that period for three to five nights. Care for him at 4:00 A.M. as usual if he should wake."

After four or five extremely unpleasant nights he slept through the 1:00 A.M. "crying" time. We let that gel for two weeks, then removed the 4:00 A.M. feeding. Fairly soon, with a few predictable mishaps, the little guy and his parents were over their sleep disorder.

THE CASE OF THE INVADERS

"We have four kids," a delightful Christian couple said. "There is no way for us to spend time together as a couple, let alone talk." They loved God, loved their children, and were exerting great energy to do right things. However, in my office, it was obvious that this well-meaning couple was teaching their children the skill of intrusion.

As the mother tried to talk to me, six-year-old Susie tried to interrupt every few seconds. Mom told her to wait, but Susie persisted. She whined, cajoled, and tugged at Mom's skirt. Mom was determined to not give in, at least for a few moments. Finally, unsuccessful at breaking in, Susie formed her hand into a paddle, reared back, and slapped her mother sharply on the face. Mom was shocked. She demanded, "Susie, you know better. What do you want?" If it works, it happens again.

Mom and Dad tried an experiment in removing the benefit. They scheduled a nightly ten-minute talk time at 7:30 P.M. One night they calmly gathered their children around them and announced:

> "Group, your mother and I are going to have a ten-minute talk time. We would like no interrupting during this period, at all. If you should intrude, we will not talk with you until our ten minutes is up. OK, we'll talk to you in ten minutes."

That night, the first three minutes were fine. The next seven were horrible. Fighting kids asked for a referee . . . hungry kids asked for food . . . inquisitive kids asked the time . . . hygienic kids asked for toothbrushes and shampoo. The parents were amazed that their children could not go through ten minutes without intruding. They resolved to remove the positive consequences and stop rewarding the interruptions.

They repeated the procedure daily, refusing to let interrupting "work" for their children. Within six days the interruptions dramatically decreased.

THE CASE OF THE "DIALOGUING" DAUGHTER

I call it "dialoguing." You have seen it. It's very popular with teens. It looks like this:

Ann: "Dad, I can't believe it. Rhonda just called and invited me to spend the night at her house this Saturday. Can I go? Please? Jenny is going, too."

Dad: "No, Ann, we have already talked about this Saturday night. It's the night before the Sunrise Service. We agreed. No out-of-the-house activities this Saturday night."

Ann: "I know, Dad, but this is special. I want to be friends with Rhonda and Jenny so bad. And they finally invited me ... me ... finally! You and Mom say you want me to have Christian friends. Rhonda and Jenny are great Christians. This is my big chance. I've been waiting for this for months. Please, I can't miss it. It's my big chance!"

Dad: "Wait a minute. Who says this is the last chance to get in with these two girls? If they invited you once, they will invite you again."

Ann: "Dad! How do you know they will invite me again? I just know they are going to invite Kathy Jenkins if I don't go. You don't understand. You never understand! You never change plans ... you and Mom are just plain rigid! You don't care about me!"

Dad: "We are rigid? We never understand or change plans for you? Let's talk about this. I recall changing our minds last weekend when we let you go skating. We bought you a new car. Isn't that caring? Let's calm down here. You're exaggerating."

Ann: "I am not calming down! I am not exaggerating! You never listen to my side! All you care about is going to church! There is much more to Christianity than that!"

Dad: "You think church attendance is all we care about? ..."

The "dialogue" can go on and on. Ann brings up new points and Dad discusses them. Ann's tone and volume steadily increase to a disrespectful pitch. Finally, she's explosive and rude. Dad continues to politely debate specific points. He wonders why Ann argues so.

This Christian father is actually teaching his daughter to angrily banter and challenge him. He may not give in and let her go, but Dad's actions send the message:"Ann, it's all right for you to bitterly badger. You may verbally assault, over and over, and I will gently answer."

Let's apply this skill of removing the benefit. My wife and I often role-play this scenario in parenting seminars. She plays the excited then angry teenager. I am "Dad." After we enact the scene, we change the script. I incorporate the present skill, remove the benefit, by changing the fourth line. I simply say:

> "Ann, I know these friendships are very important to you. I can see that you really want to go. However, this is not the right weekend. You cannot go this time."

As Judi (Ann) begins to plead passionately, I (in the role of Dad) say not another word. I just calmly look at her. Even though Judi is only an actress in a role play, "Dad's" silence is powerfully disarming. There is no one to argue with, no hostile object to push against. Her badgering power evaporates. Remove the positive consequence, and the behavior stops.

THE CASE OF LATE-NIGHT CHARLIE

He is three years old, and he is cute. His name is Charlie. He's got the biggest, darkest brown eyes on the block and he loves Mom and Dad. In fact, he loves them so much that he dislikes being away from them at bedtime. It's like clockwork. Every night, about three minutes after being tucked in, Charlie asks, "Mom, may I pwease have a dwink?" Who could say no and deprive this sweet child of life sustenance? Shortly after Mom brings him the drink, she hears, "Mommy, could I pwease have one more hug?" It would be absolutely cruel to refuse so tender a request.

One day sweet Charlie's parents realized the little requests had stretched into a nightly forty-five minute ritual. They talked about it and resolved to "Just say no." Thereafter when he requested, Mom or Dad stuck their heads in his door and gently said, "No, Charlie, it's time to sleep. Good night." Those words quieted Charlie for about three minutes—until his next request for a "dwink," and the forty-five-minute ordeal persisted.

As the nights went on, Charlie's parents sounded less gentle as they answered his requests for drinks, hugs, and prayers, "No, Charlie, don't ask for anything again. Go to sleep, now!" Still the ritual went on.

What is the problem here? Is Charlie deprived of necessary parental contact? No. Although sometimes a plausible explanation, lack of attention is not the problem here. In this case, Charlie's parents spend regular quality time with him.

The problem: If it works, it happens again. Though Charlie's parents have shifted from giving cups of water to giving cold reprimands, his requests still "work." He still receives contact with Mom or Dad—on demand. Even though it is sometimes negative, Charlie's nagging requests are always eventually followed by a benefit, *parental contact.*

Parental contact is certainly not a bad thing. Time spent with children is right and wholesome. However, Charlie is learning he is in control of Mom and Dad. They must come when he nags. The requests continue because the benefit continues.

Let's apply the skill. Let's remove the benefit. Application in this case is the same as with Nathan's monsters. After initial prayers, hugs, and kisses his parents say:

> "Charlie, we're going to the living room now. When you call us to come and give you a drink of water or to say prayers or whatever reason, we will not answer or come to your room. You have had your water and hugs and prayers. We love you. Good night."

As sure as Charlie's eyes are brown, you can bet he will call for contact in all of his usual ways. But if there is no positive consequence (response from parents), the calling will finally die out. The absence of positive consequence will do its teaching, guaranteed.

However, some "Charlies" not only call out, they *come* out. "She won't stay in her room at bedtime" is the cry of many parents. Usually, the benefit that keeps that behavior going is the same as Charlie's—parental contact. And the discipline skill of choice is the same as well: remove the benefit. For example: If four-year-old Carla's parents will preannounce their plan, then consistently resist eye and verbal contact and wordlessly lead her to bed with hand on shoulder, then she will eventually stay in bed. (Carla's parents may also preannounce and then completely ignore her as she roams. This too will eventually work.)

A FEW MORE CASES

These are the examples where removing the benefit was useful:

- Nathan's monsters
- 1 A.M. feedings
- Interrupting
- Dialoguing
- Charlie's continuing calls

Here are a few other situations where removing the positive consequences is usually very effective:

Whining requests:

Make eye contact but do not say anything or grant the request when a six-year-old whines. (Explain the procedure to your child beforehand.)

Rude demands:

Many times I have heard visiting teens use our phone and say something like, "Mom, come get me and take me to soccer." No "hello," "please," "thank you," or even "good-bye" is uttered. The parent at the other end of the phone is in a good teaching position. If that parent, after some prior explanation, will simply say, "I will not be involved with rude demands," and then hang up, the problem behavior will not last.

Temper tantrums:

Some tantrums are maintained by what occurs immediately after them. Parents may suddenly sound nicer, children may be hugged, parents may stop asking for chores to be done, or a child's demand may be received. In such cases the benefit must be discovered and removed. To remove the benefit, leave the room or wordlessly go about business as usual. (Other skills from forthcoming chapters may also be used.)

As useful as removing the benefit may be, sometimes this particular skill is not the right tool for the job at hand. When a problem behavior is a strong habit, the absence of positive consequence works but takes too long. What if his parents remove the benefit and Charlie persists in calling out for forty-five minutes each night for five weeks?

Sometimes a parent simply cannot remove the benefit. Maybe Johnny's school friends laugh and like him better when he tells off-color jokes. Mom and Dad cannot make those friends stop laughing. And limiting his social contacts at school may not be possible.

Sometimes, a behavior may be openly defiant (a ten-year-old cheating at school) or immediately dangerous (a three-year-old playing in the street). Other tools besides the absence of positive consequences will be needed. The next two chapters are devoted to those tools.

NOTE

1. This true story about Nathan and the monsters vividly illustrates the principle under-der discussion. In Nathan's particular case, we found no evidence of substantive causes of his fear. Some children do have long histories of fear; others genuinely experience syndromes such as Nightmare Disorder or Sleep Terror Disorder. Some children have nighttime fears rooted in frightening realities they endure in their waking hours. In cases of recurrent and/or extreme fear, seek competent Christian counseling assistance.

1. Some forms of behavior need to change for the good of your child. Identify one such problem behavior for each child. Write down what you perceive is the benefit that needs to be removed.

2. Some forms of behavior also need to change for the parents' well-being. Identify one behavior of your child that has a negative impact on you or your spouse. Again write down your child's benefit that can be removed.

3. Temper tantrums can be especially tricky. Have you ever resolved them in such a way that you actually encourage more of the same? How can you alter this?

4. Pick the most important behavior where a removal of the benefit would help. Now plan a five-day period of withholding the "reward" that keeps it going. Record your progress.

CHAPTER THIRTEEN

TEACHING CHILDREN TO STOP: CORPORAL PUNISHMENT

Sandra is four years old. Twice, she has ventured out the front door and across the street to visit with Mr. and Mrs. Smith. The Smiths are like sweet, doting grandparents. Their faces burst into smiles when they see Sandra. They seriously instruct her not to visit without telling Mommy, slip her just one little cookie, and escort her home.

The benefits of Sandra's trip—adoration and goodies—could easily be removed. Mom and Dad could (and will) speak with the Smiths and ask them to firmly turn Sandra away. If Mr. and Mrs. Smith immediately and consistently walk Sandra back home with no cookies and TLC, Sandra eventually will stop her travels. However, the stopping would be dangerously slow. It is unsafe for four-year-old Sandra to cross the street, even once more. Sometimes, removing the benefit is effective but too slow.

Jeremy is ten and very gregarious. He is handsome, has wavy brown hair, and loads of friends. At school he is popular, but some of his friends are profane. Jeremy begins to swear. His parents want him to stop. Can they remove the benefit? Hardly. His classmates snicker and give those subtle signs of approval when Jeremy uses just the right profanity. Jeremy's cursing provides a positive benefit that his parents cannot easily remove. Sometimes removing the benefit would be effective, but parents may have little or no control over the positive consequence.

When removing the benefit is too slow or impossible, we need a different skill to teach them to stop. That skill is the application of negative consequences. The underlying logic of this tool is as follows:

If the negative consequence outweighs the benefit, the behavior will stop.

Sometimes we must apply negative consequences to teach children that things go badly when they do wrong.

There are two types of negative consequences: corporal punishment and logical consequences. We will consider both types, corporal punishment in this chapter and logical consequences in the next.

CORPORAL PUNISHMENT

First, let me clearly define what I mean by corporal punishment. Then we will address:

- When to use it
- How to use it
- With whom to use it

The Definition

Corporal punishment is:

A negative physical consequence that suppresses behavior.

By "negative physical consequence," I mean an unpleasant physical experience—a spanking that hurts. I believe in the value of corporal punishment, but of all my parental responsibilities, it is far and away the activity I like the least. Spanking is grievous. Nevertheless, it is an invaluable teaching tool. I also do not like pain, but it too is an invaluable teaching tool. A child touches a red-hot stove, feels searing pain, and pulls away at once. The pain tells him that he is in danger of major tissue damage. "Remove hand at once!" Pain is a warning, a deterrent to danger.

With no sensation of pain, we would inflict great damage on our bodies via fire, sharp objects, or extreme weight. Physical pain is a part of God's good design—an effective warning system. Corporal punishment is also part of His design, created to warn the little ones we love: "Do not continue in this behavior; it will harm you."[1]

Look again at our definition. Corporal punishment is:

A negative physical consequence that suppresses behavior.

Note that corporal punishment "suppresses behavior." Corporal punishment is for suppressing . . . slowing . . . decreasing . . . stopping children's behavior. Corporal punishment is not designed to bring about new behavior. (Another parenting skill for that purpose is the topic of chapter 15.) Corporal punishment is for getting rid of certain behaviors, not for teaching new behaviors.

Most of us have fallen into the trap of trying to punish our children into new behavior. Perhaps we have tried to punish a child into picking up a toy, going to sleep, or cleaning a room. Spanking a child to teach a new behavior is using the wrong tool the wrong way. It does not work. Spanking may occasionally bully a child into doing something, but that "success" was likely accidental and spawned negative side effects. Punishing a child into doing is dangerous. Punishing into doing creates power struggles and can lead to child abuse. Use corporal punishment to teach a child to stop cursing, kicking, lying, stealing; do not try to spank a child into picking up toys, using the potty, doing homework, or saying "please."

WHEN TO USE CORPORAL PUNISHMENT

When should I use corporal punishment? for which problem behaviors? The question is valid. The guideline is as follows:

Use corporal punishment only in cases of dangerous or knowingly disobedient behavior.

Dangerous Behavior

One day we walked our three-year-old Jonathan out to the edge of the front yard, looked at that granite curb, and said:

91

"Jonathan, do not go past that curb and into the street without us. You could be hurt badly by cars that don't see you. If you go out into the street, we will stop you and spank you. What will happen if you do go into the street?"

Jonathan's response indicated that he clearly understood.

Later that day, Jonathan was playing in the front yard. Judi and I were on the front porch, talking and watching him. He walked toward our quiet residential street. We froze and watched. No cars were coming. Jonathan went to the curb, paused for a long time, then stepped off into the street. When his foot hit the pavement, I was already halfway across the yard. I firmly called to him, "Jonathan, no!" My loud voice and pounding steps halted him. I gripped his arm, took him immediately to his room, and spanked him.

I used corporal punishment in that situation because Jonathan had placed himself in danger. I did not want him to "find out the hard way" that playing in the street could be painful. Other examples of dangerous, corporal-punishment-worthy behaviors would include:

- A five-year-old annoying or teasing a dog
- An eight-year-old climbing onto a roof
- A two-year-old climbing out of a safety belt while the car is in motion
- A three-year-old leaving the house unannounced

In my estimation, corporal punishment is designed to be a swift and forceful teacher with immediate impact. I do not want to use a slower and less painful form of discipline when the welfare of a child is at stake.

Disobedient Behavior

Corporal punishment is for dangerous or purposefully disobedient behavior. We have addressed "dangerous"; now let us consider "purposefully disobedient." Corporal punishment is not for spilling milk, dropping the vase, forgetting, or anything accidental. Corporal punishment is for deliberate, knowing disobedience:

- When he uses a string of curse words
- When she visits Susan's house after school and you had told her not to
- When he throws away his "F" paper and tells you he got a "B"
- When she cheats on the spelling test by copying from her neighbor
- When he hits another child and takes their toy[2]
- When you tell her to put the crayons away and she defiantly throws a handful of them into your face

Corporal punishment for mistakes is cruelty. Corporal punishment is reserved for intentional disobedient choice.

Still considering the question of "when" to use corporal punishment, let us consider the guideline once more:

Use corporal punishment only in cases of dangerous or purposefully disobedient behavior.

Although corporal punishment should be used only for danger or disobedience, it need not always be used on such occasions. Corporal punishment is not mandatory for either dangerous or purposefully disobedient behaviors. In some situations where corporal punishment could be used, another teaching method may be more effective.

Corporal punishment is an intense and dramatic teaching tool. It should not be overused. Overuse can lead to physical harm, or it can teach a child to dread the presence of his or her parents. Overuse can also cause corporal punishment to lose its potency. It can be rendered ineffective by indiscriminate overuse.

Parents need to have a whole host of teaching tools for the wide variety of discipline jobs they face. I want you to be well equipped with many options. Then, I want you to be able to choose the best teaching method for the particular situation. (By the end of the discipline section of this book, I believe you will have a variety of options for teaching children to stop certain behaviors, start other behaviors, and a strategy for deciding which tool to use when.) Corporal punishment is but one legitimate option for teaching a child to stop.

HOW TO USE CORPORAL PUNISHMENT

Corporal punishment is a negative physical consequence that suppresses behavior. It should be used only when behaviors are dangerous or purposefully disobedient. Let us consider the "how" of corporal punishment. How should it be used?

- With clarity
- With consistency
- Without delay
- With an instrument of safe impact
- Without anger

With Clarity

Corporal punishment should only be used after a behavior has been clearly defined as wrong. If the child has no idea that what she did was prohibited, she should not be spanked. Such "surprise" discipline is cruel, not educational. Remember, discipline is teaching, and maximum clarity around corporal punishment enables children to maximally learn. Clearly specify that a certain behavior is prohibited and will result in a spanking. Then make sure your child understands.

With Consistency

This point follows naturally from the previous idea on clarity. If a parent says that corporal punishment will be the result of lying, that parent should keep his promise. Inconsistency is confusing, cruel, and sometimes dangerous.

Mrs. Jones clearly informs her five-year-old son, Johnny, that he must stop pulling the dog's tail. Mrs. Jones further specifies that pulling Fido's tail will be followed by a spanking. Then she sometimes spanks and sometimes ignores Johnny's dog-tail pulling. When Mrs. Jones spanks Johnny, she teaches him to stop pulling Fido's tail. When she does not spank, she accidentally teaches him to continue tail pulling. (She allows Johnny to be reinforced—it's fun to pull Fido's tail and see him run.) So sometimes Johnny learns to persist in behavior that eventually will bring him spankings. This is cruel to Johnny (not to mention Fido), and it's dangerous in terms of dog bites.

Without Delay

Corporal punishment should occur as immediately as possible after the problem behavior. Telling three-year-old Sarah in the morning that her father will spank her when he returns home in the evening will not work. A general rule applies here: The younger the child, the more immediate the corporal punishment must be. (This rule applies to all discipline.) Three-year-old Sarah does not have the cognitive ability to associate afternoon spanking with morning misbehaving. In her case, the corporal punishment must immediately follow the infraction. But nine-year-old Nina stole $10 from her girlfriend's house two days ago. You did not find out until today. She is old enough to know that today's spanking is for two-day-old stealing.

With an Instrument of Safe Impact

Pain is a teaching tool, a useful warning of further physical danger. To teach well, corporal punishment must hurt—some. However, if corporal punishment is painful to the point of damage, it is no longer a teaching tool. If corporal punishment causes tissue damage, it becomes the danger rather than the warning. This is a counterproductive perversion of corporal punishment.

In order to find the balance between impact and safety, I recommend no more than three firm swats to the child's posterior with a wide paddle. Three swats is enough to sting and provides a safe limit. A child's buttocks is sufficiently sensitive to allow the stinging sensation and is also relatively free of fragile bones or organs. A flat paddle hurts but runs minuscule risk of tissue damage when used in accord with the other prescriptions of this chapter.

In our home we started with a Ping-Pong paddle. As our children grew, we graduated to a paddleball paddle. Both instruments delivered a safe but "meaningful" swat. In addition, the use of a paddle (versus a hand) slows the process and encourages parent calmness.

One additional point. I believe it unwise to remove children's clothing during corporal punishment. Leaving clothing on avoids possible and unnecessary humiliation. Also, any potential sexual connotation that might accompany nudity is safely avoided. A paddle will still sting through clothing, and the back of upper legs can be used if very thick diapers are worn.

Without Anger

It is absolutely imperative that corporal punishment be administered without anger. Proverbs 29:15 teaches the ultimate goal of corporal punishment: "The rod of correction imparts wisdom." The purpose of corporal punishment is to give children wisdom (wisdom is knowing and choosing God's will in a given situation). Now consider Proverb 29:11, "A fool gives full vent to his anger, but a wise man keeps himself under control." A person venting anger is foolish. Can the fool teach wisdom? Angry, vengeful corporal punishment does not teach wisdom. A raging parent does not teach a child to act wisely. A controlled parent can impart wisdom.

Hostile anger is not a part of biblical discipline. It is dangerous. It harms children. Anger can fuel blows from moms and dads that rip children's skin, break their bones, and crush their spirits. Boisterous, demonstrative, adult anger damages children. We must strive to extract it from our discipline.

> Everyone should be quick to listen, slow to speak and slow to become angry, for man's anger does not bring about the righteous life that God desires. (James 1:19–20)

Yet, discipline without anger is hard. Days are long, and children are challenging. How do we get the anger out of discipline? While a mammoth task, it is worth the striving, and there are helps available. These will be addressed in later chapters.

Before leaving the "how" of corporal punishment, let us briefly address what a parent should do immediately after giving a spanking. Should the parent stay, leave, express love, wait for the child to speak? Frankly, different authors and parents disagree on the specifics. But this common point is shared by virtually all: There should be some form of positive relationship overture from the parent after the corporal punishment. By this, the parent is saying that the punishment is over and the relationship has been restored.

Some authors advocate that this be done immediately. I think this immediate association of punishment and affection can be confusing. But more important, immediate parental affection asks the child to make an immediate shift from receiving physical punishment to returning warm affection. I believe this often asks too much. I much prefer to calmly discipline and then calmly leave, saying that I will be back in a few minutes so we can talk. This gives the child time to cry, calm himself, and be ready for reconciliation. Upon returning, words of gentle entreaty to behave differently in the future and expressions of love and caring are usually well received.

WITH WHOM TO USE CORPORAL PUNISHMENT

Michael is fourteen months old. He started jogging at nine months (mere walking never interested him). He is curiosity on wheels. His latest hobby is "cupboard spelunking." He enters kitchen cabinets at one point and explores his way through pots, pans, bowls, potatoes, and onions to emerging a cabinet or two down from his entry point.

Mom would like Michael to stop the spelunking. She keeps telling him "No" and removing him from the kitchen. But Michael's expeditions resume as soon as Mom turns her back. Should the spelunker be spanked?

Joan is fifteen years old. She is becoming a young woman. She has outgrown dolls and tea parties but not temper tantrums. She gets angry, stomps, screams, sprints, and slams the door of her room. Will spanking cure the storming?

The behaviors of Michael and Joan are certainly disobedient. Michael's adventures can even be dangerous. These *behaviors* qualify for corporal punishment. But do these *children* qualify for corporal punishment? With whom do we use corporal punishment? The answer is as follows:

> *Corporal punishment should only be used with verbal, preadolescent children.*

The Lower Limit

Use corporal punishment only with children who are "verbal" — able to understand and use language. Use corporal punishment only when a child can clearly understand the verbal command "No." If children do not have the cognitive ability to comprehend Mom's or Dad's verbal prohibition, the resulting corporal punishment becomes capricious, cruel, confusing pain.

Children understand language just before they can produce it. The typical age of language acquisition varies, roughly between

97

eighteen to twenty- six months. This is the age range when corporal punishment becomes effective. When it is clear that he or she understands "No," corporal punishment can be used.

George was twenty-two months old. He stood erect and eyed a large, live umbrella plant. He liked to grab the big green leaves and just crush them. Whether it was the power of plant crushing, the reaction from Mom, or just the feel of crushing leaves, I don't know, but he liked to crush. One day, George moved close to the plant and reached for the leaf. Mom said, "No, do not touch!" George pulled his hand away and looked back at Mom. Then, while looking Mom straight in the eye, he slowly reached his hand toward the plant until he found a large green leaf. *Crunch,* he squeezed it. He quickly looked away and made for the other end of the house as fast as his chubby little legs would carry him. He clearly understood "No." He chose to squeeze the leaf. He was spanked.

The Upper Limit

How old is too old for corporal punishment? The earlier stated guideline helps us again:

Corporal punishment should only be used with verbal, preadolescent children.

I see preteen years as the upper limit for the use of corporal punishment. I do not think corporal punishment should be used with teenagers (adolescents).

Adolescence ranges from around twelve years to about twenty years old. Its exact beginning varies with each child. But, generally speaking, somewhere between ages twelve and fourteen, teen years begin and corporal punishment is no longer appropriate nor especially effective.

Corporal punishment is not appropriate for teens because teens are no longer children. Adolescents are in transition between childhood and adulthood. In my estimation, they are simply too adult to spank. During teen years, corporal punishment is too much like adult spanking adult, an awkward impropriety. Additionally, there is the imprudence of a male father striking a young woman on the private, posterior portion of her body.

Also, corporal punishment is less effective for teens. Teens learn differently from preteens. Preteens learn best by concrete example.Teens reason and abstract in a way that children cannot. Due to these differences, I believe very concrete corporal punishment is well suited for preteens.Teens are more cognitive as a rule, and other types of discipline fit them better (especially logical consequences, the topic of our next chapter).

A REVIEW

Let's take a step back and get the whole picture. Discipline is teaching children to behave in new ways. First, children must learn to stop the old behavior. In the previous chapter we focused on *removing the benefit* as one form of teaching children to stop. In this chapter we examined corporal punishment.

What is corporal punishment?

Corporal punishment is a negative consequence that teaches children to stop. It can teach Susan to stop crossing the street or teasing the dog. It should not be used to teach Susan a new behavior such as saying "please" or picking up toys.

When to use corporal punishment:

Corporal punishment should be used for dangerous or purposefully disobedient behavior. It is a swift, forceful teacher, a warning, a deterrent to harm. Robert is in danger of physical harm if he plays with matches and gasoline. Robert is in danger of moral harm if he lies or cheats.

How to use corporal punishment:

With clarity—To learn, the student must understand the instruction.

With consistency—To only occasionally spank is to teach that it is only sometimes wrong; at other times, it works.

With an instrument of safe impact—To teach quickly and warn effectively, the paddle should hurt but not damage.

Without delay—The younger the child, the more immediate the spanking.

Without anger—above all we must strive to grow in self-control if we are to teach wisdom without harm.

Whom to spank:

Corporal punishment should be used only with preteens old enough to understand. If corporal punishment is to teach, its pupils must be old enough to understand "No." They must not be so old as to suffer humiliation. Roughly, spanking is for children from ages two through twelve.

Most of these guides to corporal punishment limit its use.[3] If there are so many cases where we should not use corporal punishment, then there must be other ways to teach children to stop. Indeed, these are discussed in our next chapter.

NOTES

1. Virtually all evangelical commentators and authors on the subject concur that the "rod" referenced in Scripture indicates actual corporal punishment and that such discipline is therefore a biblical prescription. Examples include *Help I'm a Parent* by B. Narramore, *Dare to Discipline* by J. Dobson, the Baker commentary on Proverbs by R. Alden, the Eerdman's *New Century Bible Commentary* and the Zondervan commentary on Proverbs by E. Woodcock.

2. Many parents have asked me if spanking, a form of hitting, could possibly be an appropriate consequence for a child's hitting. Wouldn't spanking model that hitting is acceptable? A child's hitting is a reactive, angry outburst. An adult's spanking, as prescribed in this text, is a deliberate, controlled teaching behavior. The two are radically different. Therefore, spanking can teach a child not to physically vent anger. Spanking does not teach hitting by example, because it is a very different type of behavior.

3. Please note that these are not the only limits/cautions to the use of corporal punishment. For example, I believe it unwise to use corporal punishment with children who have been abused in some fashion. Also, I think that corporal punishment should typically only be administered by parents or guardians, and in private.

1. Why is spanking not a useful tool in promoting positive behavior? In what ways can spanking be misused?

2. What types of behavior does corporal punishment address effectively? What types of behavior are not appropriate for this form of discipline? Why?

3. Review the five necessities for proper corporal punishment. Where are you on target, and where do you fall short?

4. Give some reasons why spanking either a toddler or a teenager can be counterproductive. Based on the very different behavior of each age group, show how other forms of discipline would work better.

CHAPTER FOURTEEN

TEACHING CHILDREN TO STOP: LOGICAL CONSEQUENCES

Your twelve-year-old daughter and fourteen-year-old son are cleaning the kitchen after supper. They are arguing. You hope they will stop, but the quarrel gets louder. Their cut-downs get more caustic. As you listen, your anger rises. You feel like screaming, "Stop it! I'm sick of your bickering!"

Instead, you are calm but firm. You say:

> "You two are arguing instead of cooperating. You need more prac-
> tice working together. When you are done with the dishes, clean your
> bathroom together. If you still argue at that job, I'll find you another."

The arguing stops. Your discipline worked miraculously. Why was it so effective?

Chapter by chapter we have been looking at skills to teach children to stop certain behaviors. First, we considered removing the benefit; next, we examined corporal punishment. The technique used above is an example of *logical consequences.*[1]

*Logical consequences are noncorporal negative consequences
that suppress behaviors and that are logically connected to
those behaviors.*

Logical consequences, like corporal punishment, suppress or stop behaviors. But they are different in two ways:

- Logical consequences are noncorporal. A physical spanking is not involved.
- Logical consequences are *logically connected* to the behaviors they suppress. This means the "crime" and the consequence involve the same things. If you fight together while playing the computer game, neither of you may continue the computer game. If you don't put gas in my car tonight, you may not use it tomorrow night.

Spanking does not necessarily use logical connection. Ten-year-old Byron builds another small campfire in his closet and (appropriately) receives a spanking. There is not necessarily a "logical connection" between fire building and spanking. But if Byron bikes to Jimmy's house without asking, and the consequence is no bike riding for two days, that consequence is logically connected to the "crime."

Logical consequences are understood best by illustration. Some examples follow.

LOGICAL CONSEQUENCES IN ACTION

The Teens and the Too-Loud TV

You and your spouse are in the living room trying to talk. Your eleven- and fourteen-year-old sons are in the next room watching TV. The volume is cranked up to about ten decibels above federal safety standards. You can't hear each other talk. Twice you have asked them to turn it down; each time they did, but a few minutes later, it was back, louder than before.

You could yell, "Turn that thing down!" punctuating by pounding the wall a few times. That may work. To use logical consequences, you would warn once, then calmly walk into the den, turn off the TV, and say, "You may watch it again in an hour. It is too loud."

Note the negative consequence, no more TV, especially potent if the guys are in the middle of a favorite program. Note the logical connection. TV too loud: temporarily lose TV. Stated differently, abuse TV: lose TV.

The Four-Year-Old Female "Whino"

Your four-year-old daughter whines. In fact, she seems to always request by whining. This time, she is hungry and whiny. "Mom, I am hungry. Where is my lunch?" You could scold her, "Don't whine! Lunch is coming!" To use logical consequences you would say, "Christine, you are whining. I like to hear you, but I don't like to hear you whine. Go to your room now. I will call you in three minutes; then you may ask me your question—without whining." (Incidentally, Mom used a mechanical kitchen timer to mark the three minutes, and Christine waited for its "ding." Such timers should be issued with children at birth. They are essential tools for situations like this one.)

The Poolside Fights

Your eight-year-old twins are playing in the kiddie pool. They have a little raft and an inner tube. Of course, they both want the raft. Shelley screams, "I had it first!" Billy bellows, "You always grab everything first . . . selfish!" To use logical consequences you calmly announce, "If you fight, you cannot swim. If you fight again, your swimming time will be over for the day."

Fred's Infrequent Feeding

Susan and John were brother and sister, thirteen and fifteen, and they fought about everything. Every night they fought about who would feed Fred, the dog. This disturbed both supper and their mother. The parents had tried spanking, scolding, shaming, and ignoring. The squabbles persisted. Then, they hit upon a logical consequence.

First, Mom and Dad assigned the feeding to each child on alternate nights and wrote the assignments on a calendar. Next, the parents instituted this rule: If Fred was not fed, neither was his would-be feeder. If Fred was foodless, Mom would not set a place for the child whose name appeared on the calendar. That child would have to feed himself after he fed Fred.

The results were astonishing. Susan and John, who used to hound each other, no longer fought over Fred's feeding. They were absolutely silent, hoping the other would forget about the dog and not be allowed to dine. In order to keep from getting caught and giving the other sibling occasion to celebrate, John and Susan fed Fred regularly. Mom, Dad, and Fred were much happier.

Carl's Conniving Computer

Carl loves computers. He received his first computer game when he was seven years old. He was intrigued, invested, and enthralled. In fact, his emotions were wired to the game. When he was zapping the enemy and warping to new worlds, he was delighted. When he was getting zapped, he was profoundly upset. Sometimes he cried. But more often, at times of defeat, he would furiously critique the machine in angry outbursts, "This dumb thing is broken . . . It's not fair . . . That fireball didn't hit me!" His venting was inappropriate.

Carl's parents tried the following logical consequence:

> "When you vent your anger at the computer game with mean, angry words, you are not in control of your anger. You are not having fun. Every time you act this way, you will have to stop playing with the computer for thirty minutes."

It worked.
What makes logical consequences work so well?

THE POWER OF LOGICAL CONSEQUENCES

In the previous examples the negative consequences were directly tied to the problem behaviors:

- TV too loud: lose TV privilege
- Whine to Mom: have to be away from Mom
- Fight in pool: leave the pool
- Don't feed Fred: don't get fed
- Angry outburst at computer: lose computer

The logical connection between the infraction and the consequence is an effective teacher, because it involves something important to the child. If children are misbehaving, they are misbehaving about things important to them. They are playing TV too loud because they want to hear and see their favorite show.

106

They are fighting about the raft because having the raft, just now, is superimportant.

We humans choose to do what is important to us. And we learn best about those important things. There is a "readiness for learning" about things that matter. (How many people without flat tires read tire-jack instructions? People don't take Lamaze classes when they are not pregnant.) If he loves the computer, using it as a teaching device heightens the effect of the negative consequence. He learns faster. He gains control of his angry outbursts more quickly. Logical connection maximizes the learning because of heightened interest.

The effective logical connection between consequence and crime is God's design. Not surprisingly, the Scriptures are replete with logical consequences. To name a few, if a person stole a sheep, he had to repay four sheep (Exodus 22:1). King David took another man's wife, and later his wives were taken by insurrecting Absalom (2 Samuel 12:12). King Uzziah entered the temple of God egocentrically, sacrilegiously, and unlawfully. He was immediately stricken with leprosy, precluding any visit to the temple for the remainder of his life (2 Chronicles 26).

CREATIVE CONSEQUENCES

Logical consequences are certainly not new to parents (if you don't eat broccoli, you don't eat dessert). But increased creative use of them will revolutionize your parenting. Here are additional examples that may stimulate your creative juices and help you find more uses for logical consequences.

SLAMMIN' SALLY

The Problem:

Sally is thirteen and still has tantrums. When she gets mad, she whirls around, runs to her room, and slams the door.

The Consequence:

Mom and Dad sat down with Sally and announced that if she slammed her door, she would lose her door—for ten days. Well, she slammed it, and she lost it, along with some pride and privacy. (Dad unhinged it and put it in the garage.) The loss paved the way for learning more anger control.

YUCKY FOOD

The Problem:

Eleven-year-old Herbert had developed the habit of griping about the meals his mother prepared. Today was no exception—he didn't like the cuisine. "Oh, yuck, not this stuff again!"

The Consequence:

Removing Herbert's food and his place setting, Dad said calmly but firmly, "Herbert, your mom should not have to hear such rude remarks. Please leave the kitchen, now. You can eat later, alone."

GOOD MORNING AMANDA

The Problem:

Amanda was nine and not a morning person. On Saturday she was up early to watch cartoons. Neither eye was quite opened as she felt her way down the hall. Mom greeted her. Amanda ignored the greeting, found her way to the den, and snarled at her brother to vacate her favorite chair.

The Consequence:

Mom said, "Amanda, go back to your room. In fifteen minutes you may come out and try to treat us more civilly."

CAR PROBLEMS

The Problem:

Grandma is taking Jane and Joe skating. They are in the backseat of her car, bickering big time. She repeatedly tells them to stop—they continue.

The Consequence:

Grandma pulls over alongside the road and stops the car. "Grandma, what are you doing?" Grandma replies, "I'll wait here until you stop fighting."

THE PLASTIC PERPETRATORS

The Problem:

They were brothers, seven and eight, and they left all sorts of plastic toys in the front yard: tricycles, bats, wagons, and tents. Mom and Dad took turns nagging, scolding, or punishing in efforts to teach these guys to put away outdoor toys; the toys remained.

The Consequence:

One morning Mom and Dad sat down with these leavers-of-plastic-toys. They calmly explained:

> "Beginning this evening we have a new rule about toys in the yard. When you come in for supper, you are to bring in all of your toys (guns, bikes, everything). At suppertime we will check the yard. If there are toys left out, we will pick them up and bring them to the corner of the garage. Any toys we put there will stay in the garage for one day. You will not be able to play with them on the following day."

That night, when the boys came in, Dad scanned the yard. Not surprised, he found the usual complement of toys. He gathered all of the playthings on his way in to supper (instead of nagging the boys to pick up). He put all the toys in one corner of the garage. At dinner, he calmly announced that all the plastic toys in the specified location could not be used the following day. If the problem recurs, Dad will up the number of days the toys are inaccessible.

THE ROCKING CHILD

The Problem:

It's breakfast. Michael is fourteen, and he is leaning back in his chair. Mom could remind him for the 932nd time or . . .

The Consequence:

Mom could calmly say, "Michael, you will have to stand up the rest of the meal."

THE BOX

I would like to give you one last example of a logical consequence: "The Box." The Box is unusually effective with preteens and teenagers who leave "stuff" around the house.

Jake was nine and always left a trail of trucks, planes, and Legos behind him. He was involved in one play project after the next. Mom was in the habit of reminding him to pick up. In this way, she was responsible for his behavior. He did not have to be responsible. He left the toys and let Mom function as his memory.

One day Mom initiated a logical consequence: The Box.

"Jake, when you leave toys around the house and go off to play elsewhere, I will pick them up. I will put them in The Box in my closet. You may have them back in two days."

(Different moms and dads have used The Box with variety. Sometimes their children have to pay a small fee to receive boxed items. Sometimes, chores are used to earn back toys, etc.)

Joe is Jake's sixteen-year-old brother. He does not leave toys around. He leaves clothes. Again, Mom has taken over Joe's role of responsibility. She either reminds him (nags) or just picks up the clothes herself.

Mom produced another box for Joe:

"Joe, when I find your clothes around, I will pick them up. Then, I will put them in The Box in the garage. If you can't find something you want, you'll probably find it there. You will have to clean and iron any clothes you find in The Box. I will launder only what I find in the hamper."

Most "Joes" will pay little attention to this calm announcement— until they are looking for their favorite jeans one school morning. One such morning, Joe found his favorite jeans and T-shirt wrinkled and smelly. They were in The Box under a heap of his nasty underwear and sweaty gym clothes. That fateful morning Joe could not wear his jeans. Even worse, later he had to wash them. This was a new experience Joe did not want to repeat.

Logical consequences work, and *they have positive side effects.*

EXTRA BENEFITS OF LOGICAL CONSEQUENCES

Logical consequences reduce power struggles. Rather than pushing a child into picking up, being kind, or feeding the dog, logical consequences allow the parent to pull out of the power struggle and let the consequences do the teaching. Using logical consequences reduces the angry struggles of attempting to force children into certain behaviors. First, parents state the undesired behavior and its consequence. Then, if the child does not behave appropriately, he simply reaps the consequence. There is less personal struggle; positive relationship is preserved. On the way to the skating rink, Grandma need not nag to stop the backseat bickering. She just pulls over and waits.

Logical consequences teach responsibility. Logical consequences allow children to choose and then experience consequences, positive or negative. "If you choose to put your clothes in the hamper, I will wash them for you. If you choose to leave them on the floor, you will have to dig them out of the box and launder them yourself."

The *overresponsible* parent could continue to remind Joe to pick up his jeans. She is frustrated with his irresponsibility, but all the while she is enabling it. (If it works, it happens again.) When a child is allowed to choose a negative behavior and then reap a negative consequence, he learns to avoid such choice in the future. This means the child is learning to make better choices. The child is learning responsibility.

Logical consequences teach respect for others' limits and wishes. If Mom does not want to hear guttural groans of "Oh, yuck, not this again" after she has worked to prepare dinner, then that wish should be respected. If Dad does not want to see primary-color plastic trikes and toys in the front yard, that wish should be regarded.

The basis for the request of all logical consequences is respect for others: "I don't like hearing you fight over kitchen chores" and "I don't like hearing you fight in the pool" and "I don't want the TV that loud." After all is said and done, the parents own the house, the yard, the pool, and the TV. The children have these items as gifts on loan from parents. Parents' wishes should be respected as children enjoy the use of these privileges.

I am not advocating parental selfishness. The child's role is not to live solely for his parents' happiness. But a child's relationship with parents is his training ground for all future relationships (including his relationship with God). If children do not learn how to successfully live with us, they will not successfully live with others. An enormous part of successful relating consists of respecting the limits and the wishes of others. Selfish violation of others characterizes the worst of human behavior: infidelity, thievery, verbal and physical abuse, incest, rape, and murder. The consistent application of logical consequences to small, everyday issues teaches profound lessons of respect for others.

AN EXERCISE IN LOGICAL CONSEQUENCES

You have just read many examples of logical consequences. Now, it's your turn to try your hand. For the following two problems, you create the logical consequence. There are many "right" answers. You can compare your ideas with sample answers that follow.

TV TYRANT

The Problem:

Josh is fourteen and can be rude. He is watching TV when his little sister walks in front of the screen. He lets her have it: "Get out of the way, Sharon! You little brat!"

The Consequence:

_____

_____

SLEEPY SAM

The Problem:

Sam is seven and likes second grade. He just does not like getting up each day to go to second grade. Every morning it's the same routine. The alarm sounds at seven o'clock and Sam turns it off. Then Mom comes in and cajoles him to arise. By the third maternal visit, Sam opens both eyes. Next, Dad takes over. After a couple of his wake-up attempts, Sam is verbal but still horizontal. Finally, it gets late, Dad gets angry, and Sam gets up. Mom and Dad want Sam to stop sleeping in.

The Consequence:

_____

_____

ANSWERS TO THE EXERCISES

TV TYRANT

The Consequence:

"Josh, turn off the TV. When you treat others poorly while watching the TV, you lose that privilege."

SLEEPY SAM

The Consequence:

One evening, Mom and Dad made this announcement:

> "Sam, after your alarm sounds at seven, one of us will come in to wake you. But you are then on your own. If you are not up and ready by 7:30, this is what will happen. Dad will put your clothes in the car, and he will pick you up asleep and put you in the car, also. You will have to dress yourself in the car or face your car pool friends in your PJs."

Mom and Dad meant it, and Sam believed it. They also knew he was rather shy about being seen in his jammies. Amazingly, Sam woke, dressed, and ate ahead of schedule the following morning. (Less dramatically, but probably also effectively, his parents could have set bedtime thirty minutes earlier each time Sam was not dressed by 7:30 A.M.)

NOTE

1. This parenting skill was popularized by Donald Dinkmeyer and Gary McKay in the *Parent's Handbook, Systematic Training for Effective Parenting.*

1. Describe one extremely effective consequence that you have used (or was used on you).

2. If consequences and sin are directly connected in Scripture, then what about your own life? How has God taught you through logical consequences, and what has been the result?

3. List two particular behavioral issues with your child that lend themselves to this method. Write out what would be the appropriate logical consequences. Be as creative as possible.

4. As you actually employ these methods with your child and see some results, make sure that you refer to the extra benefits of reduced power struggles, increased responsibility, etc. Where has the most progress been made?

CHAPTER FIFTEEN

TEACHING CHILDREN TO START: UNDERSTANDING REWARD

We can teach our children to stop—to stop squabbling, whining, cursing, or leaving dirty socks around the house. But how do we teach them to start—to start picking up, saying please, doing homework, doing dishes, washing cars, hanging towels, or having devotions? How do we teach them to do new things? When I was eleven years old I began to learn the answer to this question.

My family lived in south Florida. We had the thickest, fastest-growing, most mower-bogging grass in the world. Mowing was my weekly sentence of hard labor, and I went to extremes to avoid the long arm of the law.

One day when I could hide no longer, Mom caught me and asked me to cut the grass. Just then some friends called. They invited me over to play. I pleaded my case. Mom said I could go—*as soon as I cut the dreaded backyard.* What seemed like minutes later, the backyard was cut and I was on my bike, zooming to the friend's house. I can remember thinking, *Boy, the backyard never cut so quickly.*

When I was eleven, asking me to cut half of the yard and then immediately rewarding me with a trip to play with friends was a brilliant teaching device. I worked rapidly without my usual procrastination or complaining because:

Children learn to do new behaviors by receiving positive consequences for small steps.

POSITIVE CONSEQUENCES:
PEOPLE LEARN TO DO THROUGH REWARD

People of all ages learn by reward. What happens when a baby says that first grunt or groan that may be a word? Parents, siblings, aunts, uncles, and especially grandparents go wild with excitement. The child is barraged with volumes of smiles, cheers, and high-pitched praises. The accolade would feel wonderful to anyone of any age. Will Baby "talk" again soon?

First-grader Susy carefully prints the letter "A" on her three-lined paper. Her teacher walks by and says as she posts it on the board: "Susy, what a fine job! Class, look at Susy's paper." Will Susy work dutifully on printing in the future?

A lonely teen benchwarmer visits a church at a senior team-mate's invitation. Upon entering, he is warmly greeted by the fellow ballplayer as well as two other guys and a friendly girl. They invite the newcomer to sit with them and to lunch afterwards. He feels the unmistakable inclusion. Will he be back?

People repeat behaviors that are followed by positive consequences. People learn through reward. Parents teach through reward. George comes in from school, and Mom asks him to put away his book bag. He does so. She says:

> "Thank you, George, not only for cleaning up but for being so pleasant when I asked you to put away your books. Come here, I have a special snack for you today."

Is George more likely to comply again tomorrow? He is learning obedience and some cleanliness, not to mention respect for another's wishes.

When a behavior is followed by a positive consequence, it is strengthened. In other words, the chances of its recurrence are increased; it is being learned. Or—as we said earlier—if it works, it happens again.[1]

- Letting Sharon watch TV only after she completes her homework is teaching her to work before play.

- Handing Mikey the orange juice only after he says, "Please," increases the chance that he will say, "Please," in the future.

- When teen Johnny nervously speaks to Jenny that first time in the lunchroom and she smiles and converses, his success will probably lead Johnny to try it again. He is learning how to relate to the opposite sex.

- When Mrs. Smith thanks her husband with words and kisses after he surprises her by drying the dishes, chances are he will help again. If the process continues, she may soon have a regular helper.

GOD'S WORD ON POSITIVE CONSEQUENCES

Notice that the Word of God is brimming with the concept of reward. We conservative Christians often downplay this biblical theme. Perhaps we avoid it for fear of encouraging selfish motives for serving Christ. In order to emphasize sincere and loving devotion, I think we have come dangerously close to unfaithful biblical interpretation in our de-emphasis of reward. I encourage you to use your concordance or subject index to study the theology of reward. I have been shocked to see how frequently God rewards. Here are a few examples:

- We will be rewarded for resisting temptation (James 1:12).
- We will be rewarded for obedience to His Word (Deuteronomy 5:29).
- We will be rewarded for doing good to our enemies (Matthew 5:46).
- We will be rewarded for discreetly giving to the needy (Matthew 6:4).
- Paul pressed toward the goal to receive his prize (Philippians 3:14).
- We are told that our labor for the Lord is not in vain and that each one of us will be rewarded according to his/her own labor (1 Corinthians 15:58 and 3:8).
- We will be rewarded for every good work (Ephesians 6:8).

GOD'S WORLD ON POSITIVE CONSEQUENCES

A quick look at God's creation reveals that He has ordained and liberally uses reward to teach His children to do His will. It is God's will that humans eat to survive. Why didn't He make food taste terrible and ask us to eat three times a day out of obedience? He did not. He designed immediate reward for "eating obedience." Food tastes good.

God commanded Adam and Eve to multiply and fill the earth. Did He make sexual union distasteful drudgery? No. To the contrary, there is immediate and intense pleasure in doing His procreative bidding.[2]

The point: God uses positive consequences to motivate His children. Parents have been teaching with rewards for eons. I believe it is wise to study and understand this principle as thoroughly as possible as we seek to teach our children.

THREE TYPES OF REWARD

Children learn new behavior through positive consequences. Parents are often unaware of the thousands of positive consequences right at their fingertips, ready for use. Positive consequences come in three categories:

- Personal Reward
- Tangible Reward
- Activity Reward

Personal Reward

Personal reward consists of social affirmations such as:

- Words of appreciation
- Nonverbal expressions of appreciation (smiling, winking, etc.)
- Physical affection (hugging, high fives, etc.)

Personal rewards are the most readily available reinforcers, *and they are the most powerful.*

Mom says to her five-year-old: "Jimmy, get dressed. We are going to take Dudley for a walk." Before sixty seconds pass, Mom comes into Jimmy's room and sees that he has both shoes on. She says: "Jimmy, you surprise me by how quickly you get those shoes on. That's great!" Her verbal praise and tone of voice are personal rewards for Jimmy. He responded quickly, and things went well for him.

You may remember that "Love-Hunger Skill Number Two" was to *Catch Them Doing Good.* Using personal reward as a teaching tool is very similar. This means the skill is uncommonly powerful. It does two jobs at once. Personal reward satisfies love-hunger and simultaneously encourages children to repeat the behaviors that are being appreciated. (Then the behaviors can be further affirmed, paving the way for more love-hunger satisfaction and more behavior repetition, ad infinitum.)

There are countless ways to socially reinforce desirable behaviors in children. Remember, personal rewards are the most potent. Here are a few examples:

WORDS OF APPRECIATION

- Good
- That's right
- Excellent
- Exactly
- Good job
- Good thinking
- Thank you
- Great
- I like that
- I love that
- That's interesting
- You've worked hard on that
- You really pay attention
- Show this to your mother
- Let me tell you what Jimmy did today
- That was very kind of you

NONVERBAL APPRECIATION

- Smiling
- Winking
- Nodding
- Making eye contact
- Laughing
- Clapping
- Sitting on Jimmy's bed
- Eating together

PHYSICAL CONTACT

- Touching
- Hugging
- Patting a shoulder or back
- Holding a hand
- Having a child sit in his/her parent's lap

Four-year-old Sharon eats a bite of broccoli. Dad smiles and says:"Way to go, Sharon. You are growing up and eating all types of food, even some vegetables."

Fourteen-year-old Aaron, known to buck at broccoli, silently eats half of his portion. Dad says:"Aaron, your mom worked to prepare this food ... [I like to pause for effect, then surprise Aaron] ... and you have eaten a good portion of broccoli without any complaints. Thanks for contributing to a pleasant atmosphere at the table." Dad gives Aaron a high five.

The power and pervasive opportunity of personal reward is indescribable. Children are constantly doing small pieces of behavior we taught and like. Personal reward is constantly available. If we use it, the desirable behaviors will be repeated.

Tangible Reward

Tangible objects such as toys, money, or stars on charts can also be used to teach children to do new behaviors. In an earlier example, Jimmy quickly put on his shoes when Mother asked him to get ready. Mother could easily add tangible reinforcement. Surprising him, she says:

"Jimmy, when you do what I ask so quickly, it really helps me. I think you deserve some payment for such help."

With this she plunks a quarter into his piggy bank.

Mom used personal reward and then added a physical object, the quarter. Monetary tangible rewards are used widely in our culture. We enjoy paydays. It is simply good preparation to use them wisely with our children. Tangible rewards may be:

- Money
- Food
- Toys
- Clothing
- Gas for the car
- Hobby items (tools, telescopes, pets)
- Tokens of various types

Billy and Bobby eat a little and fight a lot. Mom promised these two preschoolers a dessert if they did not say any angry words to each other during lunch. She was using tangible reward.

Nathaniel loves baseball cards. Dad told Nathaniel he would buy him a new pack of baseball cards for every ten bags of raked leaves.

Susan likes ballet but practices infrequently. Dad said Susan could have the new ballet slippers she wanted after she practiced twenty minutes of dancing for ten days.

USING CHARTS AND TOKENS

Tangible rewards can be terrific teaching tools. But always doling out money, toys, or edible goodies is obviously impractical, indulgent, and/or fattening. A new airplane model each time Richie does homework won't work. But Mom and Dad can make a chart. Eight-year-old Richie gets a check mark for every fifteen minutes of correctly completed homework (maximum one per day). After earning five checks, he receives the model, previously purchased and put away.

Charts are useful reinforcers. They give children immediate tangible reinforcement without the awkwardness of constantly handing out actual items. Almost four, Jason occasionally soils his pants. A bathroom chart with big red X's for each time he uses the potty steadily taught him to do better. For every three checks he was surprised by a small treat. He knew a treat was coming, but he liked the surprise of the occasional snow cone, story, or small toy. (The requirement of three X's was gradually adjusted to more X's until the chart was no longer necessary—but more about teaching internal motivation later.)

Tokens offer the same advantage of tangibility and immediacy. Tokens are easily handled objects given for desired behavior, which may be traded, later, for actual rewards. Tokens may be cardboard tickets, slips of colored paper, clothespins, poker chips, or plastic buttons. Like chart checks, they can be given immediately.

Also like charts, they offer children a tangible record of encouragement. The sight, sound, or feel of the growing number of checks, stars, or plastic buttons is a tangible lesson of success to a child.

> "I have seven big red buttons in my pocket," says Johnny. "I must be saying, 'Please,' a lot today. I'm improving."

Preteens are tangible learners. They learn best with physical doing, touching, or seeing. They are less conceptually oriented than teens. Using immediate, tangible reward is the treatment of choice for preteens.

Tokens and charts can also help *parents* be more consistent teachers. One clever mother was teaching her eight-year-old twins to play peacefully together. She cut slips of blue poster board and carried them in her pocket. Whenever she noticed the twins playing nicely near each other (instead of fighting over toys and the like) she gave them each a blue "ticket." Five tickets could be redeemed for a frozen yogurt bar any time after lunch and before 4:00 P.M. Mom found that using the blue tickets *helped her see and remember to reward* desired behavior (and she could reward instantly, anywhere, anytime).

Activity Rewards

Wesley is ten. His yard has pine trees; therefore, his lawn has pine cones. Not being fond of picking up pine cones, Wes usually moans about the chore and proceeds with amazing unhurriedness. But Wes loves pitching baseballs. When his dad says, "Wes, after picking up pine cones, we'll throw the ball," he moves with newfound speed. Pitching is an activity reward for Wesley.

Activity rewards are simply activities that children prefer, things they like to do. Any child's preferred activity can be used as a reward for any less preferred activity. Wesley's preferred activity, pitching, is a reward for a less preferred activity, picking up pine cones.

Next to verbal appreciation, activity rewards are parents' most readily available rewards. For a catalog of activity rewards, simply watch your children. Observe what they choose to do. Those preferred activities are all potential rewards.

- Sitting next to the window in the car
- Running errands
- Making cookies
- Swinging
- Staying up late
- Seeing a movie
- Watching TV
- Playing a game
- Drawing a picture
- Playing baseball
- Decorating the Christmas tree
- Going to Kiddie Land
- Studying with a friend
- Hearing a story

All of these preferred activities can be used as rewards to teach desired behaviors. In other words, *whatever a child is choosing to do can be used as a positive consequence to teach a child something that he is not choosing to do.* Activity rewards have been used for hundreds of years, but they can be used more wisely and creatively than we can imagine.

Six-year-old Adam is choosing to eat his mashed potatoes, but he is not choosing to eat his peas. Using activity rewards, we can say, "Adam, enjoy another bite of those mashed potatoes, but before you do, eat four peas."

Sharon and Darrell, ten and twelve, were in the midst of a favorite game when Mom arrived with the groceries. Dad used activity rewards. "Sharon and Darrell, I want you to finish your game, but before you play anymore, go help Mom with the groceries. Then get back to the game ASAP."

A FEW MORE ACTIVITY REWARDS

Notice how activity rewards are so ever available in the following examples:

- I will take you to soccer practice as soon as you sweep the garage.
- After you wash and vacuum your mom's car, you may use it.
- Brush your teeth and wash your face before you go over to Caleb's house.
- Before you spend Grammaw Joy's birthday check, write her a thank you note.
- Homework must be complete and correct before any TV.

REWARDING COMBINATIONS

Of course, types of rewards can be combined. One Saturday morning Dad stepped into the garage with cleanup on his mind. Nick and Ned, nine and eleven, were playing there, semioccupied and semibored. "Guys, I would like to play some soccer with you, but first we have to do twenty-three minutes of garage cleanup."

Dad gave them specific tasks and then used all three kinds of reward.

Personal reward—During and after the work he thanked his sons and complimented them on quick diligence.

Tangible reward—When finished, he surprised each with $.75.

Activity reward—He followed through on his soccer promise. They all played for about thirty minutes.

The guys learned, not consciously but definitely, that industry and obedience end well. Their obedience will be repeated.

Clothing Allen

To teach five-year-old Allen to dress himself in the morning, his mom devised a plan. First, she posted a large chart in his bedroom.

She told Allen that each morning when he put on his underwear and socks he would get a big red check in the top box. For putting on pants and shirt he could earn a second check mark. A third could be earned for shoes. When he earned 15 checks he could go to Kiddie Land.

Mom used all three types of reward.

Personal reward—She came into Allen's room every few minutes at first, complimenting him on his progress. Also, at dinner she often told Dad, in Allen's presence, about how well he was doing. (Such indirect praise is unusually potent.)

Tangible reward—As soon as Allen had completed the task, Mom recorded the big red checks. (He would call, "I'm ready for another check," if she was not yet there.)

Activity reward—Allen went to Kiddie Land.

Fourth-Grade Marbles

Mrs. Smith taught fourth grade. She had a small glass vase sitting on her desk next to a bowl of marbles. When all the class was working quietly she would ask a student to transfer a marble from bowl to vase. When the vase was filled, every three to five days, the class would receive an extra recess period.

The teacher, Mrs. Smith, wisely combined tangible/token rewards (marbles) with activity rewards (an extra play period). For extra fun she chose a different student each time to drop the marble in the vase—also an activity reward.

Realizing the rewards around you and their tremendous teaching power will revolutionize your ability to teach children to do desired behavior. Remember, there are three types of reward:

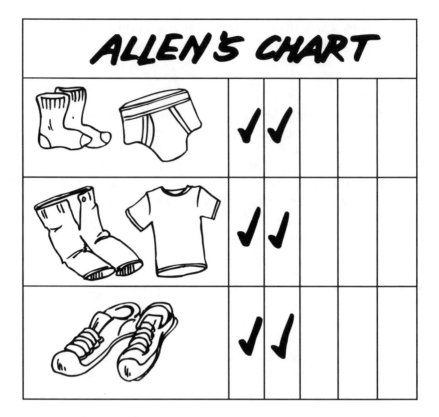

- Personal Reward
- Tangible Reward
- Activity Reward

To help you remember, use the acronym PTA. But there is more. *How* and *when* to apply positive consequences makes all the difference. The how-to of reward is the focus of our next chapter.

NOTES

1. Much of the material in this and the next chapter is adapted from two useful books, *Living with Children,* by Gerald Patterson, and *Parents Are Teachers,* by Wesley Becker. Both are published by Research Press.
2. I am sadly aware that in our fallenness we have brought some degree of ruin to all His good gifts, including sexuality. Yet, as planned, and still experienced in large measure, doing God's procreative bidding is immediately followed by positive consequence.

1. Rewards are built into both God's Word and God's creation. How have your children been a reward from God to you? How have you been rewarded by training them up to be godly?

2. Observe again the long list of verbal, nonverbal, and physical ways you offer your children personal rewards. Check off those you do consistently, infrequently, or never. How can you improve, since all of these are important for your child's growth?

3. In terms of tangible rewards, make a commitment over the next two weeks to measure and reward your child's growth in some visible way—for example, a chart with stars with some kind of treat as a reward.

4. What activities that are both beneficial and fun might you use as a reward for good behavior? Consult your children on this question and have a fun discussion. (Please take notes.)

CHAPTER SIXTEEN

TEACHING CHILDREN TO START: USING REWARD

Reward is a tremendous teaching tool. But as with any tool, the more the user knows about how to use it, the more useful it is. Parents should know these things about using reward:

- What to reward
- When to reward
- How often to reward

WHAT TO REWARD: SMALL STEPS

As mentioned in chapter 11, we don't teach children to talk by asking them to learn tongue twisters like "Peter Piper picked a peck of pickled peppers." No, parents start more humbly with words such as "da-da" and "ma-ma." We teach in small steps.

People do not learn large, complex behaviors. One at a time they learn the small steps that make up complex behaviors. People do not learn calculus. They learn to count fingers, then add numbers, subtract, multiply, divide, do fractions, decimals, algebra, and geometry. Finally, by learning hundreds of tiny steps, they learn calculus. People learn in small steps.

The first rule for using reward is to divide the desired behavior into small steps. Then reward each step along the way.

If we wait to reward her until she can say the Peter Piper tongue twister, she will never learn to talk. The mom of the previous chapter taught Allen to dress himself by rewarding small steps. She told him to dress. One minute later she was back:

> "Allen, you have already put on your underwear and T-shirt. Great job. I'm going to put the big red check on your chart right now!"

In two minutes she was back again, doing more of the same, rewarding Allen for his next small bit of progress.

Of course, this is work intensive for Mom on the front end. But *Allen is learning to care for himself.* At first, Mom is working very hard, but she is working herself out of a job.

All behaviors that we wish to teach our children can be broken down into small steps. Small steps are easy to master, and children love accomplishment. With small steps, we can begin teaching children what to do when they're very young. Four-year-old Micah can begin to learn to make his bed because he is old enough to place the pillow in the proper location. Later, he will master additional steps and eventually straighten his whole room because the small steps were rewarded along the way.

A Young Girl of Few Words

Elizabeth was a fifth-grader and had twenty tough vocabulary words to learn. Dad divided the job into small steps. Two nights before the test he said, "Elizabeth, go and learn your first five vocabulary words and come back here for a pop quiz."

She returned in minutes ready for quiz time. Dad gave an oral quiz and liberal reward. First, he commended Elizabeth for working so quickly and answering correctly. These affirmations plus special "quiz time" with Dad were potent personal rewards. Second, Dad used an activity reward: taking a mock quiz is more fun than studying vocabulary words.

Then Dad sent her to learn another five words and gave her another rewarding quiz time. She had now learned ten vocabulary words, and Dad added one more activity reward: "Elizabeth, how about showing me some of your gymnastics." A similar process was used the next night, and Elizabeth was ready for her vocab test at school.

If at any point along the way Elizabeth did not learn the five words, Dad would send her back to learn a smaller number of words, which would include the items she had missed on the quiz.

The Bedtime Slowdown

Jamey was five and slow getting to bed. He was not outright rebellious, but he stretched getting ready for bed into hours. His parents decided it was time to teach him to get into bed without the slowdown.

First, they divided "getting ready for bed" into small steps:

• Bathe
• Hang towels
• Put clothes in hamper
• Put on pajamas
• Brush teeth

Then, they focused on the last two steps, PJs and teeth, to keep the task of learning manageably small.

Next, they looked for a positive consequence that could follow the two simple steps. Jamey, like most five-year-olds, loved to hear stories. One night Dad approached him after his bath. As usual, Jamey was clad in a towel, standing in front of the mirror and making faces—part of his nightly slow-down ritual. Dad entered the bathroom with a new storybook, "Jamey, listen to this!" Dad read an exciting first paragraph and built to a crescendo:

> "And the wolves finally had the two boys cornered. They turned around with their backs against the rock. The wolves inched closer about to pounce. Suddenly . . ."

Leaving his voice and story dangling, Dad announced:

> "In exactly forty-five seconds I will sit on your bed and read more of this story. If you put on your pajamas, brush your teeth, and get into bed in forty-five seconds, you can hear the exciting conclusion."

Jamey arrived in twenty seconds flat, PJs on and teeth brushed. Dad or Mom continued this sequence for four nights. Soon, they increased the length of the behavioral chain to include bathing and bathroom cleanup.

Later, they read stories every other night and then irregularly. Mom and Dad continued fairly frequent nighttime stories. However, even when they read no story, it was clear that Jamey's compliance was becoming habit. Jamey was learning to obey and to be self-responsible. He was learning that obedience and self-care are ultimately positive.

WHEN TO REWARD: ASAP

In most instances, it is best to reward children *as soon as possible after the desired behavior.* First, let's address the concept "after." To be effective, reward must follow—not precede—the desired behavior. When desserts precede vegetables, vegetables remain uneaten. Too many of us have bargained with our children, "OK, you can go out with your friends now, if you promise to wash the car later," and have been left with dirty cars. Not only must reward follow the desired behavior, it must follow the desired behavior *as soon as possible.* When people realize that certain behaviors end in positive consequences, they repeat those behaviors. Generally speaking, the best way to associate the benefit with the behavior is to reward immediately.

Older children can tolerate more delay because they can mentally associate a specific behavior with a specific reward. But still, as a rule, immediate reward is effective reward, especially with younger children and/or new behaviors.

HOW OFTEN TO REWARD:
EVERY TIME AT FIRST—SOMETIMES, LATER

Early in learning, try to reward every time the new behavior occurs. If yard work is new for Phillip, we would not wait until his third Saturday of mowing to verbally or tangibly reward him. At first, reward each new behavior every time it occurs. Later, gradually decrease rewarding.

The effectiveness of rewarding new behaviors every time and then less frequently as they become habits is one of the most solidly researched tenets of human learning theory. To build the new association between benefit and behavior, frequent reward is a must. Once the association is solidly in place, rewarding less frequently teaches persistence. As children mature and as behaviors become habits, they accept the logic that reward is not appropriate every time. (Habits require less effort, and therefore merit less reward.)

Reward should become less frequent, but it should not stop altogether. To maintain new behavior, parents must continue occasional reward. If Simon's new behavior of hanging up his bath towels is no longer noticed, it will eventually stop. If employees never receive paychecks, they stop working. The less frequent reward should continue as long as workmen are worthy of their hire. (1 Timothy 5:18; Hebrews 6:10). To continue rewarding (though less frequently) is godly and good education.

In an earlier example, Mom was visiting five-year-old Allen's room every minute or two to verbally and tangibly reward (on a chart) Allen for dressing himself. Over the weeks it was natural to come to the room less often and finally remove the chart. But the occasional, well-placed expression of appreciation for his developing responsibility should never end.

THE DANGER OF EXTERNAL REWARD

You may be asking, as I have asked: "Will all this rewarding turn my kids into materialistic, manipulating mercenaries, obeying only if I guarantee enough goodies? With so much rewarding, will they ever learn to be self-motivated and self-responsible?" I say with confidence that teaching with rewards, according to the guidelines above, will not foster selfish, externally motivated children. To the contrary, properly used rewards teach responsibility. My confidence is based on the following two premises:

1. *Children come equipped with a God-given internalization process.*

Note the emphasized phrase in Proverbs 22:6:

Train a child in the way he should go, and when he is old he will not turn from it.

133

He will *"not turn from it"* because, as he matures, training imposed by parents becomes a part of him (or her). With growth, children take ownership of behaviors taught to them; they internalize the behaviors we have taught.

Growth in self-motivation is a natural, built-in feature, compliments of our kids' Creator. While the internalization is natural, it is facilitated by procedures outlined in this chapter, especially this one: At first reward frequently; later, reward less often. The slow and gentle decrease in positive consequences allows the child's natural internalization process to take over. The second premise on internal motivation is:

> 2. *God uses tangible, even frequent and repetitious, external reward to teach His children intangible, life changing principles.*

This truth is clear in Deuteronomy 8:3. Moses, speaking to God's people, said:

> He humbled you, causing you to hunger and then feeding you with manna ... to teach you that man does not live on bread alone but on every word that comes from the mouth of the Lord.

God used daily manna to teach His children a profound lesson of obedience. He wanted them to know there is more to life than the material world. Real life consists of hearing and obeying the God of the universe. God wanted His people to be internally motivated to listen and obey every word that came from His mouth. To teach them this intangible value, He externally rewarded their obedience six days every week for forty years. If they obeyed by gathering food in the prescribed time and amount, they were immediately, physically rewarded—they ate. God uses repetitious, external reward to teach us and profoundly change us. Using external rewards with our children can teach them internal, life-changing lessons—such as responsibility.

TRYING IT OUT

The Case of Messy Lucy

You be the "Parenting Skills Consultant." Mr. and Mrs. Smith come to you with a problem. Twelve-year-old Lucy is usually late for

TEACHING CHILDREN TO START: USING REWARD

school. She is a good student, does a good job on her homework, but leaves her books, clothes, and room in such disarray each night that finding clothes and packing books in the morning is overwhelming chaos. Her parents cannot seem to get her to clean up the night before.

Something else you should know about Lucy is that she loves the *Anne of Green Gables* stories, and this series is being broadcast next Monday through Friday on the local PBS station.

Prescribe a plan for Mr. and Mrs. Smith. (There is no one right answer for this exercise. One possible answer is given on the following page.)

A PLAN FOR LUCY

1. *Divide the task into small steps.*

_____

_____

_____

_____

2. *Devise a way to reward immediately.*

_____

_____

_____

_____

3. *Develop a plan to reward frequently at first, less often later.*

_____

_____

_____

A PLAN FOR LUCY

1. *Divide the task into small steps.*

Her parents realize that morning tardiness is caused by trouble finding things in messy mounds left the day before. They also find messiness has many elements. School clothes are strewn about as Lucy hurries out to play with friends. Later, play clothes are piled up as Lucy engages in homework. Finally, books and papers get scattered as Lucy rushes to finish and relax.

A key to teaching Lucy is subdivision into small steps of new behavior. In the past, her parents have tried to get her to clean up every night for an allowance on Saturday—too big a job for too remote a reward. This time they start with a small task. Rather than clean the whole room, her parents specify that she *pack her schoolbooks* each night. Eventually they will lengthen the behavioral chain to include other behaviors, such as putting away her clothes.

2. *Devise a way to reward immediately.*

Lucy's parents choose an activity reward that can be delivered right away. *As soon as books are packed for tomorrow, Lucy may watch TV;* she may watch the *Anne* series.

Lucy's parents videotape the series and inform her that she may watch twenty minutes each night. But her "ticket to the movies" will be the organization of school material for the following day. (Note the immediate and very frequent reward.)

3. *Develop a plan to reward frequently at first, less often later.*

During the second week, the behavioral chain is lengthened. Lucy must now clean up clothes *and* books as her "movie ticket." Eventually, other videos or even other rewards are substituted but occur less frequently. (Personal rewards, words of praise and appreciation, are used throughout, and Lucy is rewarded with less harried mornings.) In four to six weeks, Lucy will be well on her way toward developing a nightly habit of cleaning up as part of school prep for the following morning.

1. Consider the two or three areas of behavior that might be the most difficult or complicated for your child. Break them down into the smallest steps possible so that learning will be thorough, complete, and lasting.

2. Discuss a reward you have used effectively. When have you been guilty either of giving a reward preceding behavior or delaying it until far after the fact?

3. Why is it less effective over time to continue to reward the same behavior over and over? What does this do to maturity and habit formation in the child? Plan a schedule of reward for a critical behavior using these principles.

4. Why are fears of spoiling your children or making them selfish materialists through external rewards largely ungrounded? How has God made us so that this is not likely to happen if external rewarding is done properly?

CHAPTER SEVENTEEN

THE DISCIPLINE
FORMULA

The discipline skills we have considered are biblically and psychologically sound; they work. In fact, they work so well, they combine into an *If-Then Formula.*

If the formula is followed, *then* children's behavior will change. This is a bold claim. Other factors can enter in and dilute the formula, but the formula works. The Discipline Formula is as follows:

If Parents Plan and Announce
    A. Specific behaviors to be stopped
    B. Specific behaviors to be started
    C. Specific consequences to be used
And parents faithfully apply their plan
Then children will change their behavior.

Human behavior is lawful; it follows certain if-then patterns. These laws are as real as laws from the physical sciences.

If the airplane wing is curved to the correct dimension
And the airplane moves at the proper speed
Then the airplane will fly.

If the Formula is followed, children will change as surely as airplanes will fly. The power of the formula is the lawfulness of God's created order. Let's apply it to a real problem.

CHARLOTTE'S FORMULA

Charlotte is eleven. She has red curly hair, freckled skin, and lots of laughter. She is cute and winsome beyond words with a delightful sparkle in her eye—usually. But sometimes the sparkle turns to fire. With little warning Charlotte erupts in anger; furious eyes flash; bitter words spew. The explosions happen about once a day. Her parents applied the Formula. Let's look at it step-by-step.

IF PARENTS PLAN AND ANNOUNCE

The Necessity of Plans

Planning is essential, but it means work. It means stopping to focus on the problem and applying your knowledge and skill. Rob and Paula are Charlotte's parents. They, haphazardly and usually independently, tried different methods at different times to stop her anger. She continued. They decided to sit down together, assess the problem, and plan a strategy.

Discipline is a construction job, building new behaviors in children. No one would enter a construction job without carefully detailed blueprints, and parenting is far more complex than constructing buildings. We are constructing human beings. It is imperative to take time out, carefully define the problem, and specify a detailed plan.

The Impact of Unity

At this point, I pause to underline a crucial factor: parental unity. If at all possible, plan together. *The best discipline strategies will be rendered noneffective if the parents are not in harmony.* God made parents to function in accord—He made us to be one. When we are not together in our parenting, our children's lives become confusing and chaotic. One parent strictly enforces the "no running rule" at home. The other parent allows running. Which parent should be obeyed? Mom insists that vegetables be eaten before dessert. At the table, in front of the kids, Dad says, "Come on, Mom, lighten up. Let them have some dessert." The illustrations could continue: Do the kids have to go to Sunday school? Can they watch PG-13 movies? When can they date or go steady?

When one parent enforces one standard and the other condones a different standard, children learn to follow one parent and disrespect the other—always. When parents are not unified in discipline, their children are learning to disobey someone.

Parental oneness is paramount but difficult. *Becoming one* on wedding day was easy. *Staying one* in a daily way is a mammoth challenge that none of us will achieve perfectly. Yet, working to increase our unity in matters of child discipline is worth our best efforts. It will take time, energy, and the grace of God. Strive for unity as you plan and present discipline.

Parental unity or support is not always possible. Some spouses travel. Some are single. I know of no more difficult task than parenting alone. Should this be your situation, I encourage you to seek as much support and assistance as possible from the frequently absent spouse. Also, seek support and input from relatives and friends in the body of Christ. By all means, use the Formula. It will provide some needed assistance to those who must parent alone.

The Power of Presentation

There is power in numbers. Not only did Charlotte's parents plan a discipline strategy together, but they also presented the plan to Charlotte together. When the announcement of new rules and consequences can be made by both parents, together, parental teaching power is enormously increased. Parents' unified presentation has impact.

Announcement also adds clarity. Discipline is teaching, and the more clearly the material is presented, the more quickly the material is learned. Discipline simply works better when everyone is crystal clear on:

- The behaviors to be stopped
- The behaviors to be started
- The consequences that will follow

Planning and presenting together are potent. Time spent here will make untold difference in discipline. Not every discipline sit-

uation can be anticipated and planned for. But each of us can increase our child rearing planning and presenting.

What follows are the specifics of the discipline plan developed
by Charlotte's parents.

THE SPECIFICS

The Specific Behavior to Be Stopped

Rob and Paula knew that Charlotte's angry explosions were the
problem. But "Charlotte's anger" was simply too big and unwieldy
to work with. The problem behavior, the behavior to be stopped,
needed to be narrowed down to workable size. As they discussed,
it became clear that Charlotte usually unleashed her angry words
when she was asked to do something. For example:

Mom: "Charlotte, it's time for your homework."
Charlotte: "I know I have homework. You don't have to tell me every
           five minutes!"

Dad: "I would like you to sweep the back porch before lunch."
Charlotte: "Why do I have to do that? I do all the work around here!
           Why doesn't Bobby do something for a change?"

Charlotte eventually did what was asked; the surly verbal erup-
tion was the problem. Paula and Rob agreed on the specific behavior to be stopped:

Angry, sarcastic responses to parents' directives

Notice the specificity. Her parents are concentrating on one target behavior. They are not addressing Charlotte's anger toward her
brother, friends, or soccer teammates. Those are problems, and they
will be addressed eventually. But *to increase the probability of success, her parents start small.* Be specific and start small. Custer
would have won if the Indians had come over the hill one at a time.

Starting small does not mean staying small. When discipline is
effective in the one specific area, it will generalize to other similar
areas. After Charlotte learns to tone down anger at parents, she
will more easily learn to reduce pugnacious language with her soccer coach and teachers.

Before we leave the topic at hand, I would like to share a personal discovery. I have noticed that God typically deals with me specifically, one area at a time. When He is working with me—correcting, teaching, or disciplining—I have often thought, *God has known about this problem area of my life for some time, but He has waited until now to address it.* I am struck by this fact: When God is working on one problem, He is leaving other problems for a later time. He is patient and forbearing in limiting His discipline focus.

We cannot teach our children everything at once; pick a particular problem or at most two. Some problems must be put on hold.

The Specific Behavior to Be Started

Back to the story. Rob and Paula have specified the behavior to be stopped: *Angry, sarcastic responses to parents' directives.* Now they can detail the behavior to be started. What is it they want Charlotte to do instead of sarcastically venting anger? After some discussion they decided that:

> *When parents ask Charlotte to do something, they would like her to say, "Yes, ma'am" or "Yes, sir," and then comply.*

Please note that Charlotte's problem involves fairly equal amounts of behaviors to be stopped and behaviors to be started. Some discipline problems are primarily behaviors to be stopped, such as fighting or cursing. Some are mostly about behaviors to be started, such as doing homework or chores. All discipline involves stopping and starting behaviors, but sometimes emphasis of one over the other is called for.

The Specific Consequences

Once clear on the behaviors to be stopped and started, identify the consequences. Which consequences will they use to teach Charlotte to stop and which consequences to teach her to start?

Consequences That Stop Behavior

Here is the question that Rob and Paula had to ask themselves: What skills are available to teach Charlotte to stop? There are three options:

- Remove the benefit
- Apply a negative consequence—corporal punishment
- Apply a negative consequence—logical consequence

First, Charlotte's parents thought about possible benefits to her outbursts. Were there "accidental" rewards they could remove? Rob and Paula noticed that they talked and reasoned with Charlotte when she spewed sarcasm. This type of "dialoguing" was referred to in chapter 12. Hoping to cajole her into calmness, Mom and Dad unintentionally rewarded Charlotte's venting with attention and conversation.

Paula and Rob determined not to continue in such dialogue. They firmly resolved to immediately discontinue answering Charlotte's sarcastic complaints about the requested chores.

However, discipline is seldom simple. Rob and Paula discovered another benefit to Charlotte's angry eruptions. The pure pleasure of angry release was self-reinforcing. (It is simply more pleasurable to release anger than to control it.) Just letting her anger "rip" had a self-reinforcing quality for eleven-year-old Charlotte. Rob and Paula had no way to remove this benefit. For this reason, they decided to apply a negative consequence. They chose the following logical consequence:

If Charlotte angrily vents when given a chore, she will be sent to her room for thirty minutes prior to beginning the chore.

Charlotte is highly social, so the isolation should be quite negative. And she will lose the parental involvement that she gained in dialogue. If she debates (angrily or otherwise) when this logical consequence is given, her parents will maintain eye contact but speak no more words beyond firmly, calmly repeating the consequence: "Charlotte, go to your room now."

Consequences That Start Behavior

With a plan to stop Charlotte's angry words, her parents turn their attention to the goal: Charlotte's polite compliance to polite directives. They want to teach her to consistently say, "Yes, ma'am" or "Yes, sir," and then comply.[1] They choose three positive consequences:

- *When Charlotte gently complies with a chore directive, the directing parent will "catch her doing good" with verbal reward.* At first her parents will reward every time she responds politely. Later, the reward will be less frequent.
- *Also, Rob and Paula "secretly" agree to stay with Charlotte sometimes and help her when she has accepted a chore with "Yes, ma'am" or "sir."* They reason that outgoing Charlotte will like the company and the lightened chore. (This will be done fairly often, then tapered off.)
- Charlotte loves soccer and wants a new practice ball priced at $15. Rob and Paula cash $15 into thirty half-dollar coins and place the coins in a bowl on the kitchen counter. *When they catch her saying, "Yes, ma'am" or "sir," they will put a fifty-cent piece in her bank (sitting alongside the bowl of coins).*

Rob and Paula decided to announce only the third reward to Charlotte. Announcing plans to verbally praise is not necessary. They conceal their plan to assist her with chores, wisely concluding that the occasional pleasant surprise will have special impact.

FAITHFUL PROMISING

Planning and presenting the specifics of discipline is the first half of the Formula. The second half is faithful application.

If parents plan and announce
And parents faithfully apply their plan,
Then children will change their behavior.

Consistent follow-through is the all-difficult action phase. Parents must be consistent for children to learn. The announcing phase is making a promise; the action phase is keeping the promise.

Keeping discipline promises is difficult, but we have help. The Formula itself actually helps parents increase consistency in three ways. First, the Formula has helped us to narrow down to a bite-sized task. We are not trying to fix all problems at once. We are focusing on one small area. We stay more consistent when the task is more doable.

Second, the Formula increases consistency because parents planned together. Parents in agreement with each other are parents who support each other. Mutual support helps each parent follow through in the tough times.

Third, the Formula increases parental consistency because it is a public contract. Open, verbal commitment in the family context supplies accountability and helps us keep our promise. In these three ways the Formula actually helps us to increase consistency.

TAKING THE ANGER OUT

The Formula works, the Formula promotes consistency, and, as a wonderful extra benefit, *the Formula reduces anger.* Angry discipline tears down. As much anger as possible should be removed from discipline, but how? The Formula is one of the best anger-busters I know.

The Formula reduces anger because it supplies a plan. Put yourself in this situation. It's raining cats and dogs. You are in the mall parking lot, standing outside your car, holding your three-year-old, your packages, and your broken umbrella. You are late to pick up your thirteen-year-old. Frantically rummaging for your keys, you see them locked inside the car.

What is your emotional reaction? Panic! You are frantic, frustrated, and angry, unless you have a spare car key in your wallet. The spare key is your plan for just such a problem. You calmly get the key from your wallet and go on. Having a plan enables calm action instead of emotional explosion.

Without a plan, frustration and anger boil over. On the other hand, when we know what we will do next in difficult situations, we experience more calm and control. When Susie throws a tantrum, we are more likely to take it in stride if we have a procedure for tantrums.

There is a second major reason why the Formula decreases anger. The Formula diminishes the personal power struggle.

Reggie has just left the bathroom. Mom walks in and sees the soapy washcloth wadded in the corner of the tub. Her anger begins to boil. She has told him 27,000 times not to leave that wadded washcloth. Her aggravation is not because the washrag is important. It's because she has personally requested and Reggie has personally disrespected her wishes—again. She calls him into the bathroom. With red face and pointing finger, she furiously demands an explanation. Reggie reacts to Mom's rancor. He shifts into his superslow, passive anger routine. The anger in both escalates.

Let's change the scene. Mom still finds the soapy wadded washcloth, but now there is a plan in place. Mom has presented the specifics and the consequences. She unravels the rag, rinses it, and finds Reggie. "Reggie, I just rinsed your washrag and hung it in place. You owe me $1.00 as we agreed, payable immediately." She is calm. Reggie moans but pays. Why less anger?

In the first scenario there was a clash of wills. In the second scenario, *Reggie clashed with a rule.* The Formula was a buffer. Less personally affronted, Mom is less angered.

The Formula works—and it increases consistency—and it reduces anger.

If parents plan and announce
    A. Specific behaviors to be stopped
    B. Specific behaviors to be started
    C. Specific consequences to be used
And parents faithfully apply their plan
Then children will change their behavior.

THE DISCIPLINE FORMULA WORKSHEET

Back to Rob and Paula. They developed a plan for teaching Charlotte not to vent her anger when asked to do chores. They used the Discipline Formula. Step by step, following the Formula, they answered these questions:

1. What is the problem behavior to be stopped?
2. What is the new behavior to be started?
3. What will parents do to stop the problem behavior?
4. What will parents do to start the new behaior?

147

These four questions easily expand into "The Discipline Formula Worksheet." Answering the Worksheet questions one at a time will give you a clear lesson plan for teaching your children to behave in new ways. Rob and Paula's Worksheet for Charlotte is listed on the next page. They will put it into practice and modify as needed. (See Appendix B for a copy of "The Discipline Formula Worksheet," which you can use in your own home.)

NOTE

1. Slavish obedience is not implied here. It is fine for Charlotte to occasionally calmly respond, "May we talk about this?" Remember, her parents are trying to teach Charlotte polite compliance, because angry reactivity is her particular problem behavior.

THE DISCIPLINE FORMULA WORKSHEET

1. What specific behavior(s) is to be stopped?

   Angry sarcastic responses to parents' directives, especially chores.

2. What specific behavior(s) is to be started?

   Saying "Yes ma'am (or sir)," then complying.

3. What will parents do to stop the problem behavior? (Choose and explain A, B, C or any combination.)

   A. Remove the benefit.

   Parents will stop "dialoguing."

   B. Apply corporal punishment.

   None

   C. Apply logical consequence(s).

   If Charlotte vents anger when given a chore, she will be sent to her room for 30 minutes alone, prior to beginning the chore.

4. What will parents do to start the new behavior?

   1. *Parents will verbally reward, they will "catch her doing good" each time she responds appropriately.*

   2. *Parents will occasionally stay with Charlotte and help her with the chore when she responds politely.*

   3. *Parents will transfer half-dollars from the kitchen counter bowl to Charlotte's bank when she politely complies (for purchase of a soccer ball).*

IT ALL TAKES TIME

We all survived the first six weeks of parenthood—Judi, our first child, Jonathan, and I. In those weeks I had gone from rather complete ignorance to semiconfidence at being a dad. Then, it was time for Judi to edge back into part-time work selling cosmetics to the ladies in the neighborhood. She planned to go out two or three hours, a few days a week. I would come home from work and relieve her.

Her first outing was my first solo flight. True, I had cared for Jonathan by myself in spurts, but the real pilot, Judi, was always nearby. I was scared. Would I feed and burp him correctly? What if he started crying and would not stop, no matter what I tried?

That first solo was a long and shaky two hours, but I made it. Soon I graduated to three hours, and in a few weeks I could tell what his cries meant and usually knew how to handle them. I figured out how to get some chores done with him in a backpack, and I learned how to give him a bath. *I learned huge amounts about him and parenting him just by being alone with him.* Time with him was teaching me how to parent. I was learning a profound truth: time with children teaches people how to parent children. It takes time to become a parent.

Think back through the skills in this book. Each one of them takes time. It takes time to recognize, catalog, and acknowledge children's assets. It takes time to see and then catch them doing good. It takes a great deal of time to plan discipline (especially together), and even more time to explain the plans and then follow through. Every aspect of learning to parent and of parenting itself requires a significant investment of time.

Time with children makes good parents, but time with children is not enough. Throughout this book our model for parenting has been the heavenly Father. In the first section, the foundation for all love-hunger skills was the premise that our children need His love flowing through us. This cannot happen without Him at work in us. This cannot happen without time spent with Him.

Likewise, for discipline our model has been the heavenly Father. We have focused on His discipline revealed in Scripture and creation because we strive to be like Him in our discipline. Discipline is therefore a spiritual endeavor, for we cannot be like Him without Him. We cannot be like Him without spending time with Him.

Consider the time required in the summary below:

- It takes time with children to learn how to parent them.
- It takes time with spouses (and/or other helpers) to plan effective parenting.
- It takes time with children to implement effective parenting.
- It takes time with the heavenly Father to become like Him in the love and discipline of parenting.

These considerations take us to the most counterculture premise of this book: To properly parent we must take time with God, spouse, and children. This is radically counter to our modern way of rating time spent in pursuit of wealth and entertainment supreme. Even the most devoted parents are not immune from the frenzied influence of our materialistic, self-indulgent society. It seems there is no time left.

But we have no choice; parenting takes time. To find the time to satisfy children's love-hunger and teach them new behaviors, we may have to rethink our values at their core. This may mean revamping goals and schedules. It may mean different lifestyles— adjusting work hours or hobbies. It will mean being different; being people of the light, who invest time in persons that last forever.

My prayer is that you will take the skills of this book and the time so supremely necessary and train up your children in the way they should go.

A FINAL PERSONAL NOTE

Dear Reader,

We have considered some very important skills—skills that no parent should be without. But there are many more we have not touched. We have not addressed the all-important topic of meeting children's spiritual needs—making disciples in our homes. There is also much to learn about communicating with our children and our spouses. There are special concerns for parenting infants and teens; special topics such as learning disabilities, attention/hyperactive disorders, and substance abuse.

This book is not the whole picture. It is only one means of equipping. Please do not stop acquiring and sharpening your parenting skills.

Sincerely in Christ,

Bill Richardson

1. Apart from the time it takes to employ all these skills, make a specific plan as to how you will spend more time with your children over the next month. Effective behavior change implies getting to know and appreciate your children for who they are.

2. Now make a specific plan to spend more time with God. Review some material on the spiritual disciplines and study how you can change your behavior to conform to God's laws. In what ways can you achieve a fuller life in Christ?

3. Make sure that your spouse reads this book, and take some time to be with him or her to grow closer. As you become more intimate with your spouse, your parenting plans will achieve greater unity and clarity.

4. In what ways do the other distractions and responsibilities of our fast-paced life choke out the ability to gain the skills necessary to train our children? Strive for better time management to gain the time it will take to utilize all these skills.

Like the book?
Wait till you see the movie!

Child Training Techniques that Work!

The Loving Obedience
Video Series

(See back for details)

FOUNDATIONAL ISSUES

Parenting is meeting children's needs and teaching children to meet their own needs.

PARENTING:
MEETING CHILDREN'S NEEDS

"Which of you, if his son asks for bread, will give him a stone? Or if he asks for a fish, will give him a snake? If you, then, though you are evil, know how to give good gifts to your children, how much more will your Father in heaven give good gifts to those who ask him!" (Matthew 7:9-11)

In this portion of Scripture, Jesus highlighted the "giving" part of parenting. He painted a vivid picture of a parent's giving food to a hungry child. Our Lord sent this message, "As it is natural for you to meet the needs of your children, so it is natural for your heavenly Father to meet your needs." Embedded in Jesus' teaching is nestled this truth: Parenting is meeting children's needs.

This message is evident in God's Word; it is richly elaborated in His created world. Look at His design in the form and function of a woman's body. The unborn receives a rich supply of nutrients through the umbilical cord. The newborn receives all that he needs for life from his mother's breasts.

Our experience further elaborates that parenting is need-meeting. Ponder the infant you brought home from the hospital. That little one was desperately needy—desperately dependent upon you for feeding, cleaning, and warmth. She could not clothe or care for herself or even roll over. She did not have the ability to survive. She needed parenting; in this case, her needs were met.

These examples illustrate the physical needs of children. However, besides physical needs, our children have social needs. They need to belong, to be loved, and to be accepted. Social needs are real and much more than mere optional luxuries. Our children desperately need to be loved.

Our children also have profound spiritual needs. They need to know their heavenly Father. They need right relationship with Him in order to have "life"—abundant and eternal. This need unmet means spiritual death.

On all three levels, spiritual, social, and physical, our children are needy. When they are young, they cannot survive on their own. They must depend upon us, the parents, to meet their needs. Parenting is meeting children's needs. However, need-meeting is only the first part of the twofold parenting task.

PARENTING:
TEACHING CHILDREN TO MEET THEIR OWN NEEDS

Yes, meeting children's needs is a major part of parenting. But parenting is also teaching children to meet their own and others' needs.

God has designed children to grow—to develop in their ability to care for themselves and others. This development does not evolve under its own steam. Children must be taught. To be taught, they need teachers. And parents are the faculty.

> Train up a child in the way he should go: and when he is old, he will not depart from it. (Proverbs 22:6 KJV)

Parents are called to train their children. This, of course, is called discipline. Supremely important, supremely challenging, discipline permeates every parent's day. There are hundreds of thousands of behaviors and attitudes for children to learn. God tells us to train them because they need training in the billions of behaviors required in life.

Parenting is twofold: meeting children's needs and teaching children to meet their own needs. To be equipped for this twofold task, parents must be skilled in two areas: need-meeting and teaching. But who equips parents with these skills?

PARENTS NEED SCHOOL

Do Christian parents need parenting courses? Our parents didn't have Christian parenting-skills courses or books. In fact, neither did countless generations of God-fearing parents before us. Isn't the Word of God and our common sense sufficient?

Certainly, God's Word is our guide on parenting. Our common sense, our rational application to the subject, is necessary. Yet, God has clearly ordained teachers in the body of Christ and the teaching process for important areas of faith and life. The supremely significant subject matter, parenting, should be no exception. God has designed the teaching process (also called "discipling") for the equipping of the saints. Teaching on parenting is a part of the equipping of the saints—the saints who are parents. I believe it is not only allowable to teach on parenting, but it is a necessary part of equipping the church of Jesus Christ. We Christian parents need teaching for our unusually important, complex, and high calling—parenting.

CHRISTIAN PARENTS' SCHOOLBOOKS

In effect, a Christian parenting course disciples parents on how to disciple their children. It is teaching parents to teach their children how to live successfully in God's world. But what should be taught to parents? Where should we get our "parenting textbooks"—from the Word or the world? In order to be well equipped, Christian parents need instruction from both God's revealed Word and His created world.

Surely, all Scripture is God-breathed and useful for teaching and training in righteousness so that the man of God—and may I say "godly parents"?—can be thoroughly equipped (2 Timothy 3:16–17). I believe we must comb the Word of God for parenting principles. This is our supreme source and final authority.

But that authoritative Scripture tells that we can learn about our heavenly Parent from the world that He created. His invisible qualities—His power and divine nature—are clearly seen in what has been made (Romans 1:20). We can learn much about parenting by studying our Father as He has revealed Himself in creation. As Jesus taught, He repeatedly used His creation as a teaching tool. Much can be learned in the classroom of God's physical world. Systematically studying the segment of creation called "mankind" is the endeavor called "psychology." It should not be abandoned by Christians. To the contrary, we should joyfully receive and carefully examine what He has revealed in His creation. (Certainly, we must be cautious and discriminating as we consider the findings of secular psychology.) We will find treasures of knowledge when we study God's world under the supervision of our master instructor, the Word of God.[1]

So what texts should instruct us in parenting? God's special revelation, His Word, directly addresses the subject. We must use it as a prime and supervisory source. God's general revelation, His created world, under the rule of Scripture also abundantly instructs us. It, too, is our text.

NOTE

1. The use and relation of general and special revelation concerning theology and psychology has been carefully addressed in a scholarly manner by my two friends and colleagues Drs. Jim Hurley and James Berry. For a copy of their article on the subject, contact Dr. Jim Hurley at Reformed Theological Seminary, 5422 Clinton Blvd., Jackson, MS 39209.

APPENDIX
B

THE DISCIPLINE FORMULA WORKSHEET

On the following page you will find a copy of "The Discipline Formula Worksheet." By carefully and specifically answering the questions of that worksheet you will develop lesson plans for teaching your children to behave in new ways. In so doing you will utilize the discipline principles and skills previously discussed. Although the rest of this book is copyrighted, please make as many copies of this blank worksheet as you like.

THE DISCIPLINE FORMULA WORKSHEET

Child's Name _____ Today's Date _____

1. What specific behavior(s) is to be stopped?

   _____

   _____

2. What specific behavior(s) is to be started?

   _____

   _____

3. What will parents do to stop the problem behavior?
   (Choose and explain A, B, C or any combination.)
   A. Remove the benefit.

   _____

   _____

   B. Apply corporal punishment.

   _____

   _____

   C. Apply logical consequence(s).

   _____

   _____

4. What will parents do to start the new behavior?

   _____

   _____

   _____

Like the book?
Wait till you see the movie!

The Loving Obedience
Video Series

A Complete Parenting Program Ready to Use in Your...

**Home, School, Pregnancy Center,
Day Care Center, Church**

Kit includes:

- Twelve 25-minute video sessions
- A complete Presentation Guide
- A complete Promotion Guide
- Step-by-step instructions
- Handouts for every session
- Advertising posters
- Church announcements
- Interactive Exercises

Call 1-800-433-6175

If you are interested in information about other books written from a biblical perspective, please write to the following address:

Northfield Publishing
215 West Locust Street
Chicago, IL 60610